AIRFIELDS
AND LANDING GROUNDS
OF WALES: SOUTH

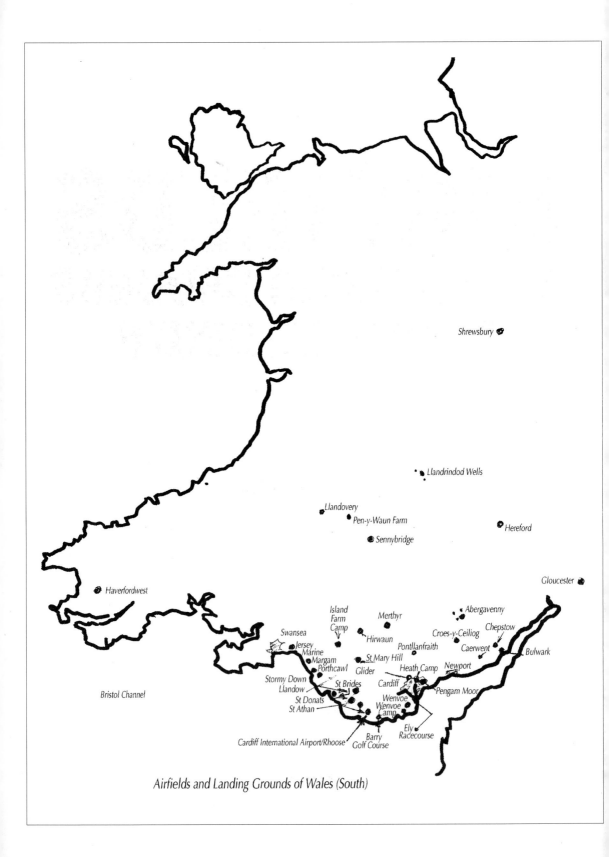

Shrewsbury

Llandrindod Wells

Llandovery
Pen-y-Waun Farm
Hereford
Sennybridge

Gloucester

Haverfordwest

Island
Farm
Camp
Merthyr
Abergavenny
Croes-y-Ceiliog
Chepstow

Swansea
Hirwaun
Pontllanfraith
Caerwent
Jersey
Marine
St Mary Hill
Bulwark
Margam
Porthcawl
Glider
Heath Camp
Newport
Stormy Down
Cardiff
Llandow
St Brides
Pengam Moor
St Donats
Wenvoe
St Athan
Wenvoe
Camp
Ely
Racecourse
Cardiff International Airport/Rhoose
Barry
Golf Course

Bristol Channel

Airfields and Landing Grounds of Wales (South)

AIRFIELDS
AND LANDING GROUNDS
OF WALES: SOUTH

IVOR JONES

TEMPUS

First published 2007

Tempus Publishing Limited
The Mill, Brimscombe Port,
Stroud, Gloucestershire, GL5 2QG
www.tempus-publishing.com

British Library Cataloguing in Publication Data.
A catalogue record for this book is available from the British Library.

ISBN 978 0 7524 4273 0

Typesetting and origination by Tempus Publishing Limited
Printed in Great Britain

Contents

Battle of Britain Day at RAF St Athan on 15 September 1962. At the foot of the picture are the airmen's barracks and the C-Type hangars of West Camp. At the top is East Camp with its Bellman hangars, and that is where the crowds are. With their cars parked as far away as the East Gate, people can be seen gathering on the far perimeter track. Note the wing of the aircraft taking the photograph, which is visible at the bottom right. (Welsh Assembly Government Archive)

Acknowledgements

Firstly I must thank the Photographic Archive of the Welsh Assembly which has put a massive amount of effort into the research for this series: Mr D. Elliot and his assistants have always been able to find and deliver interesting and evocative RAF photographs of each airfield or site that I write about. Photographs have also been supplied to me by many others over the sixty years of interest in aviation that I have enjoyed, some of whom are no longer with us.

Thanks go to D.J. Smith and Patrick Stephens for Action Stations 3. This was the trigger for my ambition to register the Welsh airfields further. Special thanks are awarded to the men who gave advice with the benefit of experience: Ken Wakefield, Roy Cottrell, Ted Chamberlain, Mervyn Amundsen, Glen Booker, Phil Howells, Ted Williams, D. Park and Tom Clement; and that fine memory of Roger Thomas who shares his knowledge with me. The public Records Office, Cardiff Central Library and the *Western Mail & Echo* have all provided data when needed. The Airfield Research Group is to be recommended to anyone who finds these pages interesting and helpful.

Introduction

This volume is the first in a series of three that records the location, history and fate of the many landing grounds, airfields, and airports of Wales. No doubt there will be some that I have missed, but a sincere attempt has been made to show anyone who is interested in aviation that Wales was definitely not excluded from the development of flight. Starting at the English border at Chepstow, and swinging in a clockwise direction around the coast of Wales because, for the most part, this was where the airfields were located, and with the occasional trip inland, the intention is to cover all of this fine country's coast, ending up in north-east Wales.

This volume covers Chepstow to Llandovery, which unfortunately for those who have read an earlier book of mine, *Cardiff Airfields*, means there is a small amount of repetition of the city's airfields. However, this could not be avoided if the total sequence of Welsh airfields was to be definitive and complete.

Included are the brief histories of the meadows, parks and golf courses that were used as landing grounds by the United States Army for their liaison aircraft, but it will be the large RAF stations in the Vale of Glamorgan, whose wartime deeds have always fired me – and I suspect most people – that will be focused on, as well as the long forgotten civil aerodromes, as they were called then, which existed in the 1930s to give trips to the people, and the air displays that moved from town to town, busy trying to make a living from this activity. This series may surprise some people by revealing that these places existed on their patch.

Ivor Jones

ONE

No.7 Satellite Landing Ground, Chepstow Racecourse

Grid reference ST 524955

This Satellite Landing Ground (SLG) opened on the remarkably early date of 1 October 1939. Landing fields were being arranged all around the country, wherever there was a chance of not only landing an aircraft but also hiding it from enemy eyes until such time as it was needed for RAF service. At this time it would need to take off again, usually in the practised hands of a pilot from the Air Transport Auxiliary, or from the Maintenance Unit that was responsible for the SLG. In the case of No.7, it began as the storage location for No.19 Maintenance Unit (MU) at St Athan, and later for No.38 MU at Llandow.

Horse racing here ceased when the Second World War broke out on 3 September 1939. The rails around the course were removed to enable small to medium-size aircraft to land and take off again. A hole in the high wall that surrounds the Piercefield Park estate was knocked out to allow aircraft that had landed to be swiftly towed by tractor through the wall. This was so they could be dispersed under the trees on the other side of the A466 road on the Oakgrove Estate. The trees on the eastern boundary of Piercefield Park were also used to hide the aircraft. The marks left by the reconstituted wall can be found today, on the north-western side of the racecourse, just south of the Piercefield Hotel at St Arvan's. The Piercefield Estate, including the racecourse, also contains Piercefield House. This may be a large, sad ruin now, but it played an important role alongside the estate in the smooth running of SLG operations during the war. The hiding of the aircraft was important and they were often hidden under the trees in specially built units. With a mixture of wire wool, wire netting, and branches used for camouflage, the aircraft were unlikely to be seen from the air. This was proven when a Spitfire of No.53 OTU at Llandow was near Chepstow when his engine caught fire. The pilot looked around for a place to land but could see nowhere suitable and was forced to crash-land in a field 2 miles away from the SLG. Although the pilot was not seriously injured, he was distressed to find out later that when he was looking for a landing place he was actually over the SLG. This proved to anyone who was interested that the camouflage of the landing ground was indeed adequate.

This lovely park was to serve not only as a landing ground but as a camp for prisoners of war, both German and Italian. It also became a barracks for successive British, Indian, and American Army units, with the racecourse grandstand serving as the quarters for the units rotating through. The Piper Cubs of the US Army's 344th Field Artillery Battalion, and

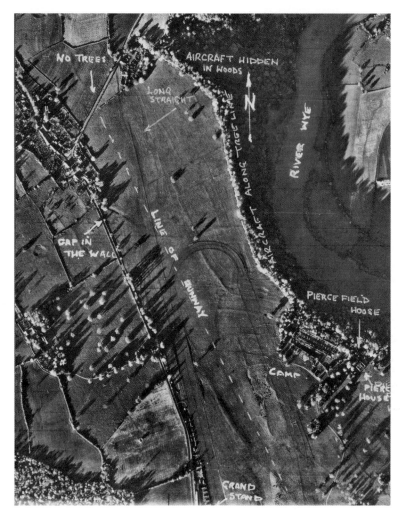

The racecourse and its environs on 4 November 1946. Over a year had passed since the last of the aircraft were withdrawn. (Welsh Assembly Government Photographic Archive)

18th Field Artillery Group of the 90th Division rotated through this camp from 1943 until July 1945. It is believed that they were here to attend the ranges at Sennybridge when they were required. They used the racecourse landing strip and as the Americans had a large camp at Chepstow many other types of US Army aircraft in service were also seen.

The documentary evidence I needed on this wartime airfield was not forthcoming at local government level, but the Chepstow Museum was able to provide me with extracts of books written by locals on facets of village histories of the area. For this I thank the curator of Chepstow Museum, Ms Annie Rainsberry. The books from which I have quoted are cited below each extract.

> By far the most dramatic development in this area however came in 1 Oct. 1939, when the Racecourse was taken over for use as a landing strip and aircraft maintenance facility. The impact on the village (St Arvan's) was obvious. A large opening was knocked into the old Piercefield wall in order to give access to Oak grove where the aircraft were dispersed against possible attack. St Arvan's Lodge was used as a boarding house for civilians working for the RAF.
> (*Fedw Villages – A history of the Lower Wye Valley*, Howell, R., 1985)

The area of wall that was demolished to give access to the fields on the other side of the A466 for the tractor-towed aircraft. (Ivor Jones)

The Satellite Landing Ground (SLG) Watch Office. Until recently this had been a dwelling since the war. (Ivor Jones)

The remains of the SLG's mess room, tractor shed, and latrines. (Ivor Jones)

During the war the racecourse was taken over as a landing ground and the fields around for parking aircraft coming in for repair and overhaul. They were stored, until required, under all the available trees around the perimeter. The RAF was in charge of this, but a number of civilian mechanics were employed to work on the aircraft. They all lodged somewhere in St Arvan's.

> The Stands, stables,and the area around the old Piercefield House were filled with troops. Nissen huts and tents were in every available space. Soldiers of many nationalities came and went. I had first hand knowledge of the comings and goings because as a paper boy until 1944 I had a permit to go any where on the racecourse as long as I was selling newspapers.
> (*Tales of the People of St Arvan's*, Edmonds, J.)

> From the Memorial Hall to the Templedoors there was an avenue of chestnut and lime trees. These were all sawn down to provide a flight path for the aircraft which were based at the racecourse. Mostly Whitley, Wellington, Boston, Beaufort, and, Typhoons. There was an army of civilians repairing them. They were housed in the village.
> (The Jones family – blacksmiths)

When levelling the runway, three huge concrete rollers were used, towed by a tractor driven by a Mr Grindell. The aim was to flatten out the bumps but when coming down the incline at the top end of the runway, the rollers overtook the tractor and pulled him down. They came to rest under the trees, and are there to this day. It is difficult to believe that so much aircraft maintenance was carried out here. There were no hangars that could have supported the idea. But there is a persistent claim that this was not just a storage facility. Lancasters arrived here at regular intervals, strange as it seems considering that this SLG started by accommodating only the smaller aircraft like Spitfires. The arrival of the Lancaster here was the reason for bringing in the extra length that St Arvan's football pitch could provide. It was also the reason for chopping down the trees on the avenue. Much of this talk about the Lancasters was confirmed to me as fact by a gentleman of eighty-three who worked for the Racecourse Co. all his working life and is spending his well-earned retirement in the Gate Lodge, at the main entrance to Piercefield Park. His name is James Dunn, and he was good enough to show me around the site of the SLG. I was shown how the line of the only runway ran at an angle to the straight mile at Chepstow, and how it crossed it halfway along its length, and also the incline from the football pitch, the flat, and its rise at the bottom end as it ran with high ground on each side at its southern end. It is surprising that wind direction was not a bigger consideration.

Jim was called up in 1939 and was away until 1945 serving with the Royal Engineers in Sicily and Italy. When he came home he returned to a job as – guess what? – nothing less than a forward airfield constructor. When racing resumed at Chepstow at Easter 1949, the rails and fences had been re-established. However, in 1960 Jim was asked to lay a runway to cope with light aircraft for VIPs. This was necessary to provide a landing ground for the racing trainers and jockeys, together with the wealthy people who attended racing. This function had been fulfilled up until then by the airfield at Bulwark, 2 miles to the south. Bulwark's fate was to be divided into two halves by a new road – the A466 – when the M4 was built, and most of the rest of Bulwark Airfield was used as a housing estate. Jim built the runway following the same line as the old runway, but this time he was confined to the inner dimensions of the race track. I am fortunate to have this on a 1963 overhead photograph.

The same rollers that caused havoc on the incline sixty years ago. The perimeter wall is in the background. (Ivor Jones)

This road lay at right angles to the aircraft's approach to touchdown in the field on the right. Trees were felled, and the wall was lowered on the right as now. Traffic was held up while the aircraft passed over from left to right. (Ivor Jones)

After touching down and running down a long slope, the line of the runway is along the middle of the photograph to the tree-line in the south, crossing the racecourse straight. Of course there were no rails here for the period of wartime use.

Remaining there is the disused building that was used as the watch office, a latrine block and the repair to the wall, but I cannot find any evidence of the usual Robin hangar. The office is exactly the same design as the usual SLG, such as at Rudbaxton and Wrath Head.

TWO

Bulwark Airfield, Chepstow, Gwent

Grid reference ST 535925, north of junction 22 on the M4

This small grass landing ground was in use before the 1939–45 hostilities and, according to people living there now, it seems that approximately 1935 was the start of its existence, to convoy race-goers to the Chepstow course – the racecourse being 2 miles to the north of the airfield – but there was no traffic control or fuel stocks. There were no hangars or shelters, but it became a popular visiting place for club pilots from Cardiff (Pengam Moors), Gloucester and other clubs.

Flying from here ceased for the duration of the war but resumed after it ended and the airfield was to see its busiest period until two instances occurred to end its life. Firstly, Chepstow Racecourse opened its own landing strip in the middle of its circuit, which had been the landing strip during the war for the satellite landing ground and the Piper Cubs of the US Army. Secondly, by 1950 the building boom to house the returning servicemen had inspired Chepstow Council to use the extensive area of farmland at Bulwark to build a large estate.

With the construction of the M4, junction 22 was inserted. Its roundabout uses land that was just south of the airfield, but the A466 that runs from this roundabout north to the racecourse and the Wye Valley to Monmouth was to cut right through the old airfield. The western part of the field remains as it was, but the eastern side is full of housing and sports fields.

It has been mentioned that the Red & White Bus Co. had some input in the development of this field. It would make sense, as their Head Office was just 200 yards away, and they had expanded their holdings, making many acquisitions all around the country, but I can find no evidence that the company was involved. There is no data at the museum or libraries about this little bit of aviation history.

Aircraft types seen by witnesses at Bulwark range from the DH Tiger and Puss Moths and Auster Autocrats, up to the DH Dragon Rapides.

Recent research by Mr Phillip Howells of Pembroke into the whereabouts of US Army units in Wales leading up to D-Day has been able to locate the 174th Field Artillery Group at Bulwark Military Camp in spring 1944. In May 1944 they were joined by the 987th FA Battalion of the 3rd Army with its 155mm guns.

The L4 Cubs acting in the Air Observation role for these many units must have used the landing ground at Bulwark, as there was little else for them to use, and it was adjacent to the camp.

Above: The airfield as it was in March 1948. The white diagonal line represents the later line of the A466 coming up from the M4, just a few metres to the south. (Welsh Assembly Government Photographic Archive)

Right: A Miles Hawk of Gloucester Flying Club, at Bulwark in 1947.

A Piper Cub L4-Air Observation Post, similar to those that served at Bulwark in 1943/44.

A couple of miles to the east of here – just over the border with England – was Sedbury where the 182nd FA Group of the 3rd Army (in March) and 690th FA Battalion of the 1st Army were housed and probably used Bulwark for their Piper Cubs. All of these artillery units were expecting to rotate in turn.

THREE

Caerwent Landing Ground

Grid Reference ST 455910, beside the A48 between Newport and Chepstow

It is impossible to find any information about this little used airfield. The usual searches in the district libraries, museums, newspapers, and records offices have been fruitless. There was just the one young farmer who recalled what he had been told of the field by his now-deceased father, which confirmed the AA register of Landing Grounds, published for the period of the 1920s and 1930s, which had been given to me by another aviation researcher and mine of information – Mr Ray Cottrell.

It is strange to read the Automobile Association's helpful hints on the use of the airfield by its subscribers:

1   The airfield is controlled by Mrs. A. Rosser, Court House Farm, Llanfair Discoed, Nr. Chepstow
2   A permit to use this field will be issued by the A.A. on payment of 2/6. Application should be made on a special form supplied by the A.A.
3   Surface—Level pastureland
4   Warning—The ridges should be avoided. Horses, cattle, and sheep are pastured
5   Telephone—Caerwent Post Office. Telephone Caldicot 37 (1 mile)
6   Fuel—Mr A. Adams, Grocer at Caerwent. Telephone Caldicot 11 (1 mile)
7   Transport—Crick Corner House Garage. Telephone Caldicot 42. (Fuel and meals can be provided) 1½ miles
8   Hotels—'The George' Moor St, Chepstow. Telephone Chepstow 365 (5½ miles)
9   Railway—Severn Tunnel Junction. G.W.R. (6½ miles)
10 Air message service boxes—11 miles N.W., 7 miles N., 13 miles E.
11 Nearest Aerodrome—Bristol Whitchurch, 17 miles S.S.E. 148 true
12 Inspection—First of every month

This is a lovely broad meadow sited on the north side of the A48, and one can understand its choice as a landing ground, but I have no evidence as to its use. Perhaps the rich man's attendance at the Chepstow racecourse for the regular meets explains it. Another small detail is that an ordnance depot was built here just prior to the Second World War, in the next field to the east. This was to become an essential US Air Force and Army Depot which was to continue up until the 1990s.

Another reason for a visit here is the Roman Camp at Caerwent and the castle of Caldicot.

The fact is that this was a registered airfield merits its recording in this book.

Above: Caerwent Landing Ground.
(Welsh Assembly Government
Photographic Archive)

Right: Looking from west to east
at the north end of the field at
Caerwent. (Ivor Jones)

Below: The airfield, looking across to
the north from the roadside of the
A48. (Ivor Jones)

FOUR

The Airstrips at Abergavenny

Many places in South Wales played host to the United States Army during the build up to the D-Day landings in June 1944, and some stayed a little longer after the landings. Nowhere was this more evident than the town and district of Abergavenny.

Playing host was not confined to the Americans; there was a large presence of British Army units here also. The headquarters for the Western Command South Wales District was at St Ronans, Abergavenny, with Major General J.G. Halsted CB, OBE, MC, as its commander. In addition to its general staff there were the A and QMG branches of the Royal Engineers, the US District Engineers, the Royal Corps of Signals, the Royal Army Service Corps, the Medical and Dental Services, Ordnance, the Royal Electrical & Mechanical Engineers, Movement Control (covering freight, personnel, RAF movements, and USA movement) and Quartering. There were very many British troops stationed here requiring large numbers of houses to be annexed for accommodation.

There were many other nationalities represented at different periods: Belgians, Poles, Indians, but the largest in number were the Americans. It is estimated that there were 100,000 US troops stationed in and around this small market town (as it was then) and it was bursting at the seams. There was a Tank Corps at Cwrt-y-Gollen, an Engineering Corps at Llanover House and grounds, the 99th Infantry Regiment at Glan Usk House, whose troops were of Scandinavian descent and were ski troops.

There were four battalions of US troops in all who spent time at Llanover Park between June and August 1944. These were the 283rd and 284th Field Artillery Battalions, 807th Tank Destroyer Battalion and 191st Field Artillery Battalion. These units were equipped with the Piper Cub L4s, Air Observation Post (AOP) aircraft, two to each battalion. The intention was to give each of these gunnery units some shooting practice at the Mynedd Epynt ranges nearby, but not all managed to get this done.

Ty-Mawr was a large house that was used to accommodate the children evacuated from a London Approved School, and in its grounds in Gilwern, some 3 miles west of Abergavenny town centre, the US Army decided to build a hospital – 279th Station Hospital – equipped with some of the best surgeons of the time and fifty-two wards plus four operating theatres. After the landings in Normandy their work really began. Those cases who needed treatment that the field hospitals on the Continent could not provide – for example skin grafts, amputations – would arrive by train at Abergavenny Station where a fleet of Army ambulances would meet them and transfer them to Ty-Mawr. There were two airstrips associated with the hospital. One was a short distance from the front of the hospital, in a field across the road to the south-west. A small field used for visitors, it is in exactly the same condition as sixty years ago, lying alongside the Cae Meldon road in a north-west to south-east direction, about 4,000 yards long (grid reference SO 245148). This field clearly could only handle the L4 Cub.

An overhead of the US Army Hospital of Ty-Mawr, Abergavenny. The smaller cub strip is to the south-west of the camp and hospital. The much larger landing ground is to the north-east (as marked). This photograph was taken on 17 June 1945; the hospital still has GI patients. (Welsh Assembly Government Photographic Archive)

The hospital built by the American Army at the village of Gilwern. Numbered 279, it served from 1943 till 1946. The smaller cubstrip is in the foreground and the larger one is at the rear of the hospital. (Bob Rivers)

The second landing ground lies to the north of the hospital. A much more adequate field alongside the river Usk, it is served by a narrow concrete road from the hospital about half a mile away. The Approved School lies between the airstrip and the hospital. This larger strip could handle much bigger aircraft than the L4 and without stretching the imagination

Ty Mawr main airfield, between the river Usk and the hospital today. The trees are of course of post-war growth. (Ivor Jones)

Left: The smaller strip in front of Ty-Mawr looking east. (Ivor Jones)

Opposite above: This is the field that was used by the Americans as a cubstrip when they were based at the camp of Dan-y-Parc. Looking to the north-west. (Ivor Jones)

too much one can visualise larger ambulance aircraft using the place but nobody can prove it now. It is in a very secluded place, and the comings and goings would hardly be noticed. It is again today much as it was then, except for the growth of many young trees. It is at least 700 yards in all directions and the grid reference is SO 260130.

Dan-y-Parc was another very large house with vast grounds situated approximately 4½ miles north-west of Abergavenny town centre, where the British built a sprawling hutted camp early in the war. The house has been demolished, but the two lodges are extant and from the gate at the lodges one can see the roads and bases of the camp. The gent who led me to these sites, Mr Goff Watkins, had himself been posted here during his time with the RAF. Many nationalities attended the camp in turn, and it was when the US Army occupied the site during 1943–44 that the field on the other side of the main road was requisitioned for the deployment of the L4s of what was probably the 177th Field Artillery Group. Half of this field is now an industrial park but the remaining part, running down a slope to the A4077 road, can still be viewed. Grid Reference SO 200170.

This airstrip is situated a mile to the to the east of Dan-y-Parc, across the river Usk, then across the A40 road to its north side and on a wedge of land a few hundred yards away from the British Army Camp at Cwrt-y-Gollen that was taken over by the US Army for its L4 AOP Cubs. It seems that by early 1943 at least a part of the barracks at Cwrt-y-Gollen had been occupied by US troops other than the Tank Corps mentioned before, because, by late 1943, the 284th Field Artillery Battalion, which was part of the 177th Artillery Group, had four of their L4 AOPs based on this tiny field that runs alongside the A40. This unit was joined by the 174th and 991st FA Battalions, and after these had left for the invasion ports, the 87th FA Battalion which arrived here for the period 13 May–3 June, joined by the 258th FA Battalion later. Apparently the field also came to be used by the Austers AOPs (Air Observation Post) of the British Army, who carried on this use up until the 1950s. It is unchanged from sixty years ago; only the trees that were an obstruction then have now been chopped down. Grid reference SO 235175.

Right: Cwrt-y-Gollen was taken over from the British army and used by several units of the US Army. This was the cubstrip alongside the river Usk. Four Piper Cubs, two tents, and a jeep can be seen at the left end of the field. (Courtesy of Mr Howell Davies via Mr Ken Wakefield)

As soon as war began in 1939 measures were taken to train young men under the age of call up in the Cadet Force, whether the ATC (Air Training Corps), Sea Cadets or Army Cadets. Many towns near the sea had their Sea Cadet hall and a boat to row or sail. Many towns had camps for the Army Cadets, in or near the barracks of the larger towns, but in most places there was no shortage of applicants for the Air Training Corps. As a result gliding schools were set up wherever possible to give these boys – who all aspired to fly a Spitfire – some air experience. The golf course at Abergavenny was to be one of these schools, becoming W6 Station, and it was staffed by No.1062 Squadron of the Air Training Corps. This is situated 1½ miles south of the town centre, between the B4209 and A4042 roads, with the river Usk forming its eastern and southern boundaries. The gliders used were one ancient Daglin and two Kirby Cadets and they were also provided with a hangar to store their gliders, towing winch and recovery vehicles. With the cessation of golf on the site, the place was cleared of unwanted obstacles, and gliding began.

1943 saw the arrival of US Army Units and, as elsewhere in Abergavenny, things had to give way to accommodate such large numbers; so the ATC was told that they must share their field with the L4s of the 58th and 87th Armoured Field Artillery Battalions. It was better than being thrown out of their field – as was done at the Glider Field at Llanishen, Cardiff, where the hangar was lost to them also. Not so here: the hangar – an Over Blister – was always the property of the Glider School. The hangar is still in use today and houses the golf club's mowers. Grid reference SO 300120.

All the strips detailed here are situated on one side or the other of the river Usk, because the river valley floor is the only flat area available, making it all the more surprising that so many landing grounds were in this lovely area.

Adding to the militaristic environment during the war was the sudden incarceration of Adolf Hitler's henchman, Rudolf Hess, in yet another large house turned hospital – Maindiff Court. He stayed here from 1943 until the Nuremberg Trials for war crimes in 1947.

This overhead of 31 August 1945 shows both Cwrt-y-Gollen on the north side of the Usk and Dan-y-Parc on the southern side. Both ex-British military camps and both cubstrips can be seen. (Welsh Assembly Government Photographic Archive)

Abergavenny Golf Club on 2 April 1946. Note the Blister hangar initially provided for the Air Training Corps and used for the Piper Cubs during late 1943–mid-1944. (Welsh Assembly Government Photographic Archive)

FIVE

The Airfield and Cubstrip at Croes-y-Ceilliog

Mon. Grid Reference ST303975

At the time of its use this airfield ran alongside the now redundant Newport road that lay north to south and was called 'The Straight Mile' by the local motor cyclists, where many a wager was made and lost. It was of grass, and was approximately 400 yards in length by 150 yards in width, flanked on the left by Graig-y-Felin wood and on the right the straight mile. It lay on high ground with all kinds of heavy industries to the west and lovely countryside to the east and is said to belong to Race Farm.

Today the new road – A4042 (T) – with its dual carriageway and deep, broad cutting, veers off to the left at the place where the airfield was, having followed alongside the old Newport road till then. The planting of trees on the ridgeline of the cutting has almost wiped out the airfield and leaves only a small wedge of grass.

There had been flying here in the 1930s and witnesses describe air shows where wing walking and stunt flying occurred, and the usual flying trips around the locality were paid for. I have failed to discover who put on these shows – the last one was in 1938. By the description given of two three-seater biplanes, I wonder if Mr Pine of Porthcawl laid on the shows.

During late 1943 units of the US Army occupied the hutted camp at the nearby New Inn's polo grounds, about half a mile from the airfield. This large camp had previously served the British army and the Indian army.

Mr Alf Lambert recalls this:

> I remember the Yanks and their two planes. They were brought by road and were in crates, they assembled them at the Polo grounds camp then towed them without wings to the airfield, and the wings were put on there. They brought the two big crates as well, and they were placed at the end of the field and they used them to work and keep out of the weather. The cabins were there when the men left for France.

Alf also recalls the airshows: 'I remember seeing the biplane taking off and landing, they were giving short flights at so much a time, and a large crowd watched'.

I have failed to find out which army unit was involved here and no records of any kind exist locally. It was almost certain that it was an artillery battalion of the 90th Infantry Division based in south-east Wales.

Croes-y-Ceiliog Airfield. The hedge has been reconstituted since the war and the new highway ploughed right through this field. (Welsh Assembly Government Photographic Archive)

This photograph shows cubstrips in Italy, but it could not have been more apt for the purposes of this book: the trees and mountains in the background are so like those of Croes-y-Ceiliog.

SIX
Pontllanfraith Camp and its Airstrip

Grid Reference ST170955, 5 miles north of Caerphilly

Situated on a heavily wooded hill, between the A4049 and the A4048, was the district of Penllwyn. It was at the time of the build up of US Army Divisions in South Wales in 1943. It had been decided that the British and Canadian Division would concentrate in the east of England, and the American Divisions in the west.

These US Units had experienced little opportunity to do the serious training that would get them ashore at Normandy, and the space to manoeuvre in these hills and valleys was a benefit.

The US Army had units all about these valleys, in small camps, littered about the small mining communities, and at Penllwyn they erected a tented camp on the slopes of the hill that is now an Industrial Park.

The camp was to accommodate the 204th Field Artillery Battalion, with its 155mm guns, in February 1944. Part of VIII Corps of the 3rd Army, they were to train at the Sennybridge Ranges when the opportunity arrived. They were joined by the 270th FA Battalion with 240mm howitzers also of the 3rd Army. When these units moved out they were replaced by the 87th FA Battalion on 13 May, only staying until 2/3 June.

None of these battalions mentioned was attached to the US divisions based in Wales but came from divisions across the border in England, and returned to them as soon as their stint at Sennybridge was completed, including the vital exercises involving the Air Observation Posts – the Piper Cub L4s aircraft that were flown in co-operation with the batteries on the ranges. Connected by radio to these, the AOPs would observe the fall of shot on target and then radio the necessary corrections to the batteries. Each Infantry Division had ten aircraft, two to each Artillery Battalion, and the aircraft accompanied their parent unit at all times.

The airstrip used by these artillery units was located 1½ miles north of Penllwyn, at a village named Cefn Forest, and the field used was the same as that used pre-war for air shows and flights for 5s. It is known as the showground as it was used for travelling fairs and the like. It is now a sports ground, a rather undulating surface, but flat areas are rare in these hills.

The site of the US Army camp at Penllwyn, Pontlanfraith, on 3 August 1945 just after clearing up. This was mostly a tented camp deployed in the woods, with more permanent hutted communal buildings on top of the hill. The concrete bases of some of these are visible. The airfield is at the top of the photograph (north) in the village of Cefn Forest. (Welsh Assembly Government Photographic Archive)

Middle: It is hard to believe now but this spot would have been the middle of the camp at Penllwyn, right on the tip of the hill facing west. (Ivor Jones)

Below: This is an attempt to show the landing ground known as the showground in Cefn Forest. Used for sport predominantly but before the Second World War it was an occasional airdrome, and 1943–45 an American Piper cub field. (Ivor Jones)

SEVEN

Military Use of Pengam Moors, RAF Cardiff 1937–45

Grid Reference ST 215770, 2 miles east of Cardiff city centre

Built from land reclaimed from tide fields and foreshore near Pengam Farm, the landing ground that had been allocated to Cardiff Aeroplane Club by Cardiff Corporation started its life in September 1931. The club flourished quite well during the years up to the outbreak of war with good membership, a club house, and hangar. Then, in 1936, the Air Ministry began their surveys into the possibility of making Pengam Moors into RAF Cardiff. By 1937 it was settled that Cardiff would be a base for No.614 County of Glamorgan Auxiliary Air Force Squadron. In Army Cooperation Command, the construction of hangars and other buildings began. Richard Cadman, the Aero Club's chairman, became Squadron Leader Cadman OC of No.614 Squadron.

The airfield was shared by Western Airways, Cardiff Aero Club and the Royal Air Force. Cardiff Aero was to act as manager of the base until the outbreak of war. In those last months of peace the club had approximately eight aircraft on charge: three Gypsy Moths, two BA Swallows (one powered by a Pobjoy engine and one with an ADC Cirrus engine), a Hornet Moth and two Tiger Moths. I have been advised that the club also had a 'Wicko', a cabin for two seats and high-wing monoplane. With these aircraft the club ran down on the advent of the Second World War.

At the end of the war the club resumed its activities, but without the same volume and interest. They had accidents as all clubs do, such as in September 1951 when the pilot of a Tiger Moth and the pilot of an Auster Autocrat, both from Cardiff, did what was described as 'dogfighting' over Dinas Powis (5 miles from Pengam). They collided with each other and fell from the sky to crash on Dinas Common. Both men were killed. The chief instructor was Mr Doug Kemp and Dennis Panes was in charge of maintenance. At this time, in the 1950s, the club was flying Hornet Moth G-ADMT, three Tiger Moths and two Auster Autocrats. Then, in 1958, Tiger Moth G-ANEV, taking off into an easterly wind and heading, struggled and then stalled, finally crashing on St Mellons Golf Course, causing the deaths of Mr Moss Eddems, an experienced pilot, and a pupil (name not known). The club carried on flying from Pengam long after the airlines and RAF had gone on 1 April 1954. The club faded away rather than died around 1957/58, eventually re-appearing at the new airport at Rhoose.

The Cardiff Ultra Light Club
This club had a brief history jammed between the end of the war and the airfield's closure. The club had a 'Tipsy' light monoplane which was fitted with a 50hp Walter

This overhead of 30 April 1959 shows the state of things just after its closure. 52 MU hangars are still evident on the mid-left of the shot. Curran's flight shed is marked and the MAP hangar above it. On the upper right the gradual destruction takes place of the old RAF site, where the two Bellman hangars appear roofless. (Welsh Assembly Government Photographic Archive)

Auxiliary Air Force No. 614 Squadron's Hawker Hectors, in section formation, fly over the Vale of Glamorgan. ('Ted' Chamberlain)

Cardiff Aero Club's Wicko aircraft at Pengam Moors in 1939. (Mervyn Amundsen)

Cardiff Aero Club's post-war Auster Autocrat – G-AHSW – at Pengam. (Mervyn Amundsen)

Cardiff Ultra Light Aero Club's Tipsy aircraft outside the east Bellman hangar. (Mervyn Amundsen)

Micron engine. It seems that this aircraft caused the death of a pilot too. On taking off into an easterly heading (again), the 'Tipsy' stalled and went down, killing Mr Preece, the pilot.

Cardiff Municipal Airport

Cardiff Municipal Airport opened in September 1931, along with the official start of the Cardiff Aero Club. Starting with the title 'Splott Aerodrome', after the Cardiff suburb on its northern boundary. The name was changed in about 1936. The area designated for the airfield was low lying and subject to flooding from the Bristol Channel/Severn estuary, therefore a sea wall was built around the airfield by Cardiff Corporation. The river Rhymney entered the Channel along the eastern boundary of the field. It was, of course, a grass airfield with not a single hard runway, and it was not until the laying of Sommerfeld Tracking for one strip that life became bearable for aircraft, aircrews and ground crews. A concrete runway was laid in the summer of 1942.

Civil Flying And Airlines

In 1932 the *Bristol Evening News* ran an experimental, twice daily service between Bristol and Cardiff for one week, using an Avro Ten, to Wenvoe Aerodrome. Later British Air Navigation ran a four times a day service also between Bristol and Cardiff (Pengam) using a Fokker F VII A, G-EBTS 'The Spider'. But this service failed to attract enough customers and fell through. Western Airways then took over the service but only running twice a day with a DH Foxmoth, G-ABYO, carrying just three passengers. Western ordered a DH Dragon for the route, which was later extended to take in Bournemouth on 17 May 1934 and further extended the service to Le Touquet and Paris on 3 May 1935.

On 2 October 1938 Western started a night service to Weston-Super-Mare from Pengam. These were the first scheduled internal night flights in the UK. Western kept these services running until the war broke out, when they were chartered for Army co-operation work.

In May 1948 the Weston-Super-Mare to Cardiff route was resumed in association with Cambrian Air Services Co. But in 1949 Western Airways handed over their share of the route to Cambrian and ceased operations completely in South Wales. 1949 saw Cambrian awarded licences for Cardiff to Jersey, Guernsey, Barnstaple, London and Birmingham. The 'Plum route' to the Channel Islands had its inaugural flight to Jersey on 16 May 1949. These scheduled routes continued until Cambrian left Pengam Moors to begin operations from Rhoose. All airline traffic ceased at Pengam on 1 April 1954.

The GWR (Great Western Railway) started an air service from Pengam to Plymouth via Haldon on 12 April 1933, after trials the previous day. It operated twice daily in each direction on weekdays until 22 May. The route was then extended to Birmingham (Castle Bromwich) and the frequency cut to once a day on weekdays, until the route was closed for the winter on 30 September. This route's attempt to make money failed but it was a success for the customers: 50 minutes to Haldon at a cost of £3 and 75 minutes to Plymouth at a cost of £3.10. GWR used the Westland Wessex.

All the railway companies, including Southern, GWR, LMS and LNER had realised that they must amalgamate their airlines to make profits, so Railway Air Services was born. Under this new company, the route Cardiff–Haldon–Plymouth and later Birmingham and Liverpool Speke, was re-introduced. On 7 May 1934 the flights were once a day in each direction on weekdays. These routes were uneconomical and the trip became Cardiff–Weston–Bristol on 25 May 1936 and the Cardiff to Weston service became hourly. These routes continued much the same until the war, and of course the Rail Air Service never returned post-war. On 31 July 1946 the routes Cardiff to Bristol and Cardiff to Weston were re-established. The Bristol route was flown six times every weekday and the Weston route no less than fourteen times in each direction daily.

Railway Air Services ceased all operations 31 January 1947. Cambrian Air Services carried on with its growing airline at Pengam Moors until the move to Rhoose in April 1954.

Military Use of Pengam Moors RAF Cardiff 1937–45

No.614 Squadron, up to its mobilisation and posting off to Odiham in October 1939, had Cardiff as its HQ. The weekend training and evening classes for ground and aircrew began to mould the group into shape. Then in October 1939 they left, never to return. This didn't mean the airfield became deserted, as different support units made their home at Pengam. Added to the arrivals and departures of aircraft for J. Currans, Air

Some of the fleet of DH Dragons at Cardiff Pengam Moors of Western Airways. (Ted Williams)

Cambrian Air Service's DH Dragon-Rapide – G- ALAT – between the two Bellman hangars at Pengam Moors in around 1948. (Ken Wakefield)

A Westland Wessex of Great Western Railway Air Service, loading near the original Cardiff Aero Club hangar at Pengam Moors. (Ted Williams)

DH Dragon of Railway Air Service's 'City of Cardiff' at Pengam Moors. (Mervyn Amundsen)

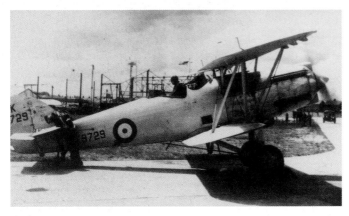

The RAF hangars are being constructed in 1938 behind this Hawker Hector of No.614 Squadron, AAF, at this station now officially named RAF Cardiff (Pengam Moors). Note the pilot is inspecting the aircraft's tailplane while his Napier Dagger engine is running. This was 1938. ('Ted' Chamberlain)

Dispatch Co. and the flown in aircraft for No.52 MU (some came by road), the field was kept fairly busy.

The aircraft carrier 'Courageous' was torpedoed and sunk by a U-boat on Sunday 17 September 1939, just a fortnight after the war started. The survivors of No.815 Squadron were reformed at Worthy Down Airfield in Hampshire, but their next operations were to be over the Bristol Channel.

The squadron, with their Fairy 'Swordfish' aircraft, flew to Cardiff Pengam Moors in January 1940 where they were to develop flying anti-submarine patrols, usually at dawn to Lundy Island and back, the idea being to keep the submarines from coming to the surface. The losses of allied shipping in the area were very high in 1940. The squadron was troubled by the wet conditions at Pengam and were unable to take off and land safely, so many patrols were missed. No.815 Squadron left Cardiff after only a few months on posting to Bircham Newton. While at Cardiff, because of the sinking of 'Courageous', the aircrews were fêted and a Lord Mayor's reception was held at the City Hall in February 1940.

No.8 AACU (Anti-Aircraft Co-operation Unit) arrived in November 1940 from Weston Zoyland to help the 9th Anti-Aircraft division in the area of South Wales in training and practice shoots. This unit had been formed just five months before at Ringway Airport, had then been sent to Weston Zoyland in Somerset briefly and then on to Pengam Moors. Here they stayed for over three years until they disbanded on 8 December 1943. They came equipped at various times with all sorts of obscure aircraft because of the shortage of serviceable modern types. Initially there were DH

Dragons, Dragon Rapides, Dragonfly, and the three types of General Aircraft Co., Monospars, the S 6, S12, and S25, and also Blenheims, Lysanders, Dominies and later Oxfords and Masters.

With the approach to D-Day, vast quantities of USAF and Army supplies were held here. The Americans had stores ready for the Continent and their C47s were to land at Pengam to pick these up as and when they were needed in France. They assembled and tested a squadron of Piper Cub L4s here and some say around a dozen of these AOP aircraft were handled. They had been shipped in crates from the US to Cardiff Docks and brought by road to the airfield sheds of John Currans, where American Army engineers assembled them. The majority of these Cubs were then flown off to the Glider Field in Llanishen and the strip at Heath Camp.

Air Dispatch Co. was doing lots of work outside their MAP contracts. Their apron was swamped with odd jobs including Beechcrafts, DC 47s, Vengeances, Thunderbolts, Avengers and even a Marauder made a landing on the 960-yard x 50-yard runway.

No.587 Squadron sent a detachment to Pengam from 10 April 1944 to 1 October 1944 with their Martinets, Henleys and Hurricane IICs. This unit had been formed at Weston Zoyland on 1 December 1943 and the aircraft were coded M4. This squadron was the result of the merging of three separate flights – Nos 1600 and 1601 Target-towing Flights, and No.1625 Anti-aircraft Co-op Flight. The squadron was

This overhead shows the five Bellman hangars, and other buildings of No.52 Maintenance Unit at the north-west corner of the airfield. It is 1948 and three years have elapsed since its closure as an Air Ministry site, but it was soon to be making the coachwork for buses and trolley buses with Bruce Coachwork, which was a development of the now defunct Air Dispatch. (Welsh Assembly Government Photographic Archive)

equipped with Oxfords, Masters, Vengeances, Henleys and Hurricane 11cs. These aircraft were all providing target practice for anti-aircraft batteries, and sometimes air to air gunnery training.

No.286 Squadron had a detachment to Pengam, at various periods between April 1942 to May 1945. Formed from No.10 Group anti-aircraft co-op training at Filton on 17 November 1941, it was simply renamed No.286 Squadron, with Oxfords, Defiants and Masters, Martinets, and Lysanders. The unit code was NW and it was disbanded 16 May 1945 at Weston Zoyland.

No.663 Squadron, No.1952 Flight, from Llandow arrived on 15 October 1949 with AOP Auster Vs and stayed until 18 June 1953 when they returned to Llandow as Pengam's flying days were coming to an end.

A famous and vital role in the Second World War was played in the five Bellman hangars of No.52 Maintenance Unit at the north-west corner of the airfield. Opening on 3 February 1940 as a crating, packaging and shipping depot for the RAF and RN single-engined aircraft that were needed in the Far and Middle East and Mediterranean war zones. The Hawker Hurricane was by far its largest customer, but the Spitfire and Seafire came close. The variety of types was endless; old biplane trainers were shipped out to the dominions to enable them to set up flying schools there.

Messrs John Curran Engineering had a large flight shed on the airfield, and a purpose-built factory to repair Bristol Blenheim bombers on the western side of Cardiff. They were to do this job under the auspices of the Civilian Repair Organisation. When the major repairs had been carried out at the main plant, each aircraft, minus its wings and propellers would be towed with its tail-wheel held on the tractor and its main

The engineering works of John Curran Ltd in Cardiff took on the contract to repair aircraft of the Bristol range during the war, the Blenheim Marks 1, 4, and V, plus the Beaufighter. In the front row a Mk IV, on the left, and a Mk V, on the right, can be seen. The picture shows the main plant and there was also a flight shed on Pengam Moors. (Mr John Davies)

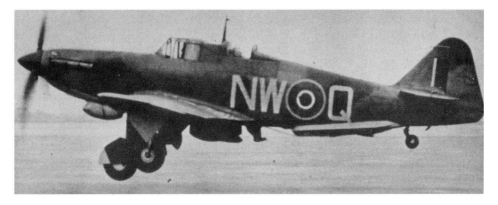

Many Army co-operation flying units flew from RAF Cardiff at various periods during the war, and No.285 Squadron was one of them. It is May 1942 and this is a Boulton Paul Defiant III target towing aircraft, serving the many anti-aircraft units along the coast. (Frank Jones)

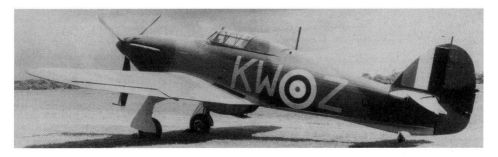

Hurricane Mk 1 L1592, KW-Z was to spend short periods at many Welsh airfields after its operational life was over. 9 Air Observer School at Penrhos 1942. 48 MU Hawarden 42/43. 52 MU Cardiff, and 47 MU at Sealand. Photographed at Cardiff's 52 MU. (Frank Jones)

undercarriage down, would proceed through the city centre to the east of the Cardiff where they would enter the flight shed to be fitted with its wings and propellors. When the war ended the work ceased, but by that time they had produced 193 Blenheims of all marks and Beaufighters, that would have probably been otherwise scrapped because of the damage sustained by the aircraft.

Another Civilian Repair Organisation that developed on the airfield was that of Air Dispatch Ltd. This company started life as a smallish airline with a DH Dragon that managed to get the contract to fly the morning English papers to Paris from Heston in London, and that was one of the many achievements of its owner – the amazing, world record-breaking, daredevil female, the Honourable Mrs Victor Bruce. She owned a fleet of twenty-three Dragons and Rapides at the outbreak of the Second World War, along with a staff of fitters and riggers to maintain them, and crews of pilots and wireless operators.

On 3 September 1939, the Air Ministry handed her a brown manilla envelope that told her that ten of her aircraft were to be taken into the RAF immediately. This had all been planned long before and other airlines suffered too.

The 1947-product of a fine company that could not beat the big boys. The bus was delivered to Cardiff Corporation Transport, after its coachwork was completed by Bruce Coachwork. They provided their many customers with superb work, but were bled white by the shortages of materials, such as aluminium sheet which was claimed by the major manufacturers.

Mrs Bruce was ordered to leave Heston and take the remnants of her fleet to Pengam Moors immediately, where her company now became the National Air Communications Unit, formed at Cardiff with the task of conveying VIPs and military brass to the Continent. This went on through the phoney war period, but when France fell the Air Ministry, through the MAP, wanted to acquire her staff and then commandeered all of her aircraft. The lady knew that her aircraft had to go, but she wanted to retain her skilled men and applied for aviation work to justify their retention.

The Air Ministry agreed and after a contract from Helliwells to repair fabric-covered wings of training aircraft was satisfactorily completed, she obtained orders to repair complete aircraft such as the Hawker Hart, Audax, and Furies that were used as training aircraft at that time. Air Dispatch did so well that her workforce stayed and were awarded more exacting work on Harvards and many other types. They also made parts for other contractors, such as cowlings and engine nascelles.

They used one of the Bellman hangars on the RAF site and the old Cardiff Aero Club hangar and the basement under a large block of apartments in Cardiff city centre that had previously been a car park. At the peak of production there were 700 workers at Air Dispatch.

At the end of the war, when other work was being sought by companies that had been doing much the same as they had, they managed to get into the coach-building business by constructing the coach work on the chassis of double-decker buses for Cardiff

Corporation and other towns under the title of Bruce Coachworks. The company did a fine job, but under the prevailing shortages of the materials needed and the economics of the large-scale production that was necessary to be profitable, the company was forced to close in the late 1950s.

The airfield at Pengam was now very quiet. John Curran was now working on radar arrays, the No. 52 MU was gone and the army co-op flights gone. Air Dispatch had also gone but another unit arrived in the form of No. 3 Reserve Flying School (RFS), and the flying club returned. In 1947 the return of Western Airways and Cambrian Air Services took up the challenge of departures from Pengam.

The No. 3 RFS was one of many across the UK, formed to maintain the flying skills of newly released aircrew, and also to teach new pupils. It was a part-time, casual activity; the CO, a retired wing commander, was also the manager of Cambrian Air Services next door. The unit was equipped with three Tiger Moths and five DH Chipmunks for pilot

No. 3 Reserve Flying School at Pengam Moors. The aircraft is a Chipmunk of that unit and the lad is Maxwell Morris. (Ted Williams)

This is the Airspeed Oxford used for navigation and wireless training by No. 3 Reserve Flying School at Pengam Moors.

training, plus two Oxfords and two Ansons for navigation and wireless training. This good idea came to an end like so many others due to defence cuts in spending; all the Reserve Training Schools were disbanded in 1953.

From 1 January 1948 until its closure in 1961, the old RAF hutted camp, built for No.614 Squadron in the 1930s, was occupied by a non-flying, civilian outfit called No.1 Fire Fighting School under the auspices and funding of the Ministry of Transport and Civil Aviation. It was an original idea and went on to great things elsewhere, but at Cardiff it started with four fire officers and four new recruits. It was a mutual attempt to do the correct thing using the correct materials, with the right equipment in dealing with airliner fires. In other words they had to 'write the book'. Britain wanted to lead the world in all things aviation for peacetime use.

The school grew and grew, bringing students from all over the world, from all countries that aspired to receive long-distance flights to their country. A large fleet of vehicles was acquired – some designed at the school – and experiments with different agents were employed: foam, gases, water, sand, and many others, until the best results were obtained.

Many scrapped, large aircraft were brought to Pengam for these trials and experiments, starting with RAF types like Halifaxes, Lancasters, and Hastings to the early DH Comets, and other civil airliners.

Each course was of one month's duration, and was fully booked each time; about forty men on each course, living as lodgers on the nearby housing estate. The permanent staff numbered ten or twelve at any one time, until 1955 when Pengam closed as an airport and everything was moved to the former RAF station at Rhoose – the new Cardiff Airport. Ten trained firemen and a few officers went to Rhoose, leaving the school's instructors, and a couple of firemen for demonstration fires, to carry on teaching the pupils, until the Rover Co. insisted on their departure as they were building a transmission plant near the school. The school packed up and left for Stansted Airport in Essex in 1961.

Yet another non-flying unit which used the facilities for some years arrived in 1945. This was No.7 Transport Company in No.54 Wing, a kind of holding unit. Formed a few months before the war's expected end, the idea was to use all the RAF lads with lots of service abroad, to come back to the UK and do something useful while awaiting their turn for demobilisation. This meant that ships, which were in short supply, would have fewer to bring home later at the war's real end. This was done in all regions but where lads from South Wales were concerned they reported to Pengam Moors. Doing something useful turned out to be the stripping of all RAF airfields, and other sites, of their removeable equipment, whether cooking and catering gear or machine tools and spares including engines. Office equipment, beds, desks and benches were all collected by this assortment of trades, including aircrew who played the part of drivers and their mates. They used a very large fleet of heavy trucks, and Queen Marys, plus the articulated heavy sets, and the stuff was transported to storage depots such as Stamford Bridge, Quedgeley, Spanhoe and Speke.

Those men who were married and had a home to go to locally did so as if they were in civvy street. Those who were not stayed in the RAF huts on the airfield. They were all demobbed, and the Welsh airfields stripped by 1947.

The old airfield is long gone and most people in Cardiff are unaware that the place that is now a housing estate was once filled with such a mighty war effort for

No.663 Welsh Flight, with its Taylorcraft Austers which arrived from Llandow on 15 October 1949 and stayed until June 1953, when they returned to Llandow as Pengam Moors was closing down. They were equipped with aircraft similar to this. (RAF Museum photograph)

Cambrian Air Service's DH Dove at Cardiff Pengam Moors in the early 1950s. This aircraft could still operate from the small and restricted airfield at Cardiff, but the time was running out on this old ground. (Ken Wakefield)

women, as well as the men, at this tiny airfield of Pengam Moors. No.614 Auxiliary Air Force Squadron did re-form in Wales after the war, but not at Cardiff. They were to form at Llandow but a fine memorial to the men who paid the price of war while with the squadron is at a site in what was the middle of the runway at Pengam.

EIGHT

Ely Racecourse Landing Ground

While the experiments with airship and airplane had been proceeding at Pengam Moors to the east of Cardiff, another place was entertaining the public with the new thrills of aviation. This was to the west of the city at the well-known Cardiff Racecourse, later named Ely Racecourse. Air displays, or exhibitions as they were called then, were held at Ely before the First World War. Gustav Hamel would thrill spectators with aerobatics in his Morane Saulnier. Hamel was famous and on 9 September 1911 carried the first official Air Mail Hendon to Windsor. His career was cut short when, in May 1914, his plane ditched in the English Channel.

Another aviation pioneer was David Prosser who also visited Ely Racecourse. He obtained his pilots' certificate (No.526) from the Royal Aero Club on 18 June 1913, flying a Caudron. These men were in the forefront of aviation even before the huge advances that the First World War was about to bring.

On 22 September 1911 the *Western Mail* reported that history had been made at Ely Racecourse in Cardiff on Saturday – and it was difficult to foresee the far reaching results of what took place!

> Mr Grindell-Mathews, the inventor of the aero-phone, succeeded under the most trying conditions in establishing communications by wireless telephony with an 'aeroplanist' careering in the air at 700ft high, in strong winds and heavy rain, and at the speed of an express train!

The most sanguine hopes of the experts on the ground were more than realised, and the inventor went away pleased. Mr B.C. Hucks, the plucky young aviator who braved the elements under conditions the majority of flying men would have deemed too dangerous, was also pleased to be the first airman to take part in wireless telephony. His fine Blackburn monoplane, the Mercury, acted splendidly in the tricky wind, and when he descended, with the telephone receivers still tied around his head, he was given a hearty cheer.

Two months previously Ely had a grand flying week, with passengers enjoying flights at £1.10 return. The exuberant *Western Mail* reporter took his first flight and stated that an interesting feature was the filming of the whole event by the Gaumont Film Co.

On the ending of the First World War many businessmen could see the advantages of air travel, and one of these was Captain Alfred Instone. He was the vice chairman of S. Instone & Co., a large shipping company that, among other things, shipped vast cargoes of coal from Cardiff to ports on the Continent and the early arrival of documents of lading to the ports on the receiving end saved time and money. Alfred describes all this in his history of the company:

The airfield without the racetrack and some of the old grandstand, and enclosures which remain at centre right. (Welsh Assembly Government Photographic Archive)

Edwin Prosser, a Welsh aviator, with his Caudron at Ely Racecourse in 1913.

Well-known aviator
Gustav Hamel with a a
Morane Saulnier at a meet
at Ely Racecourse in 1913.
He died a year later.

Grindell-Mathews
operating the ground set
of the aerophone on Ely
Racecourse on
22 September 1911
(*Western Mail*)

Another famous aviator
who attended meets at
Cardiff's Ely Racecourse:
Mr B.C. Hucks in his
aircraft, Mercury, testing
Grindell-Mathews'
aerophone in September
1911. (*Western Mail*)

We had a fleet of steamers, both our own, and time chartered, which were costing us a lot of money each day, and it was quite customary for these ships to arrive at north French ports a week or ten days before they could discharge their cargoes, owing to the fact that the bills of lading were delayed in the post. These were mostly cargoes of Welsh coal at this time.

We conceived the idea of purchasing an aeroplane and getting the government's permission to carry our own letters, which was granted, with the result that after our ships were loaded with coal the documents were sent over by plane, and the ships were consequently in a position to proceed to their berths, and discharge their cargoes immediately on arrival, perhaps a week before other vessels forced to lie off ports, awaiting the documents to arrive. This was the means of saving the company thousands of pounds in ship hire and demurrage. Out of this exercise arose the company of Instone Airlines as a separate entity, to its parent.

Instone Airline's Captain Bernard pilots the first flight to the continent for the company in the DH 4 from Hounslow on 13 October 1919 after the short trip to Ely racecourse.

> Our first aeroplane was a two-seater D.H.4 with a Rolls-Royce engine, and in October 1919 Barnard took it on its first flight to Cardiff. It returned with documents to Hounslow, London in 56 minutes. And soon after left on its first trip to Paris. The De Havilland 4 was an ex-first world war aeroplane, with the pilot occupying an open cockpit, and two passengers could be carried in an enclosed cabin behind him.

This flight was not the first connection of the name of Instone with aviation. As long ago as August 1910 the company promoted the flight of Captain Willow's airship, City of Cardiff, on a similar trip to London. This airline prospered and expanded, and was absorbed into the mighty Imperial Airways in 1924 and the flights from Ely Racecourse ceased.

I have an advertisement referring to the flying of an Imperial Airways Airliner, Prince Henry. Flying from dawn till dusk giving short passenger flights for 10s 6d, 7s 6d, and 5s. This was to last one week and the programme on Wednesdays, Saturdays and Sundays included wing walking and parachute descents. The use of the airfield for airshows began to attract all kinds of small flying circuses, such as this advert of 6 August 1920:

> JOY FLYING AT CARDIFF. Grand Flying Week At Ely Racecourse.
> Commencing Aug 7 Passenger flights in latest Avro two passenger aeroplanes from £1.1s.0d. Cross country flights undertaken at short notice.

When the Cardiff Corporation decided to draw up a town plan of their area, one of the proposals in the forefront of the scheme was provision of an aerodrome and, in 1921, the racecourse at Ely was earmarked for the purpose and embodied in the town planning scheme as an open space.

In 1927 the matter of an aerodrome became a practical policy, but it was found that this particular land was not suitable owing to its configuration around the actual racetrack. Other sites were therefore carefully examined and finally the Splott foreshore, generally known as Pengam Moor, was decided upon. In choosing this site the Corporation was influenced by the fact that, immediately adjoining it, it would be possible to develop, at little expense, a similar accommodation for seaplanes. A most desirable combination.

It only remained to purchase the land at Pengam.

NINE
Camp Heath Cubstrip

Another airfield in the leafy suburbs of Cardiff, for a short spell, was at Heath Park. When the American Army moved over here in preparation for D-Day, they occupied many sites in Cardiff. Maindy Barracks, Whitchurch Common and Heath camp were the busiest.

In the summer of 1943 ten Piper Cub L4 Grasshoppers were shipped over from the US, along with other munitions, to Cardiff Docks. After unloading these aircraft that were in a crated form, they were transported by road to Pengam Moors, where they were installed in the John Curran flight shed. After assembly by the US Army engineers, they stayed at the airfield for a few months, and were then flown off to their allocated units, including the glider field at Llanishen and Heath camp, both in Cardiff. The US Army had arrived in the early spring of 1944, at what the US Army called Camp Heath, bringing with them a Battalion of Field Artillery – they were the 892nd, part of the 90th Division, bringing with them thirty-four officers and 347 men. They were to be the recipients of at least two of the Grasshoppers for AOP (Air Observation Posts). These planes needed to have the airstrip as close to the battalion headquarters as possible, so they used the field at the northern side of the park used today as football pitches. All this was great fun for the local lads as there was no restriction on the use of the field by the public. When the 892nd moved out to the troop transports to embark, as backup assault troops, after D-day they were replaced by the 345th Field Artillery Battalion, this time of the 75th division who stayed from 14 May to 3 June 1944.

The pilots of these small planes were expert at landing and taking off in small spaces, but Heath Parks' largest uninterrupted, treeless space was still less than 400 yards and they would only just clear Heath Park Avenue's houses by a few feet.

This camp had been occupied by the British, Cypriot, and many other foreign army units before its American occupation, but once they had gone no other military unit was to stay here after the end of 1945.

Many of the camp's buildings have survived, including the parade ground, drill hall, guardhouse, commanding officer's bungalow, and the airstrip.

The field at Camp Heath today, much the same as sixty years ago. (Ivor Jones)

The Americans called this place Camp Heath when they took it over, after many other British and allied units had spent time here. This oblique shows the cubstrip on the left and the hedge line that was removed to accommodate the US Army's air observation L4 Cubs. (Welsh Assembly Government Photographic Archive)

The Guard room at Camp Heath has had many uses since the war. (Ivor Jones)

TEN
Glider Field Cubstrip, Llanishen

Yet another landing ground for light aircraft was temporarily established here during the war. This substantial area of council land was largely earmarked for housing and industrial development post-war, but at this time, 1941, it was a large, fairly flat area bounded by Ty-Glas Road (the original one) to the north, Kimberly Road and Coed-y-Cae Woods to the east, the Crystal Woods and the railway to the south. The Inland Revenue's offices and other industry such as Royal Ordnance's large site were to the west.

In early 1941 the Air Training Corps was allowed to use this area to fly off and land gliders as part of the lads' training in handling aircraft. In the beginning they relied on a saloon car to give them tows to become airborne. The car was a gift from a local businessman. Later, the ATC acquired a fine improvement as a tug. It was a mobile, barrage balloon winch, the same as the winches manned by the WAAFs around the city at that time.

The lads carried on their flying, weather permitting, and they received a visit from the famous bomber leader Guy Gibson (whose wife lived in Penarth) in 1943 to give them a pep talk. Then came the news that the unit had to move out to Pengam Moors Airfield to continue their flying from there, as the Yanks were coming.

It is believed that the Air Liaison element of the 2nd Evacuation Unit US Army, which moved into tented accommodation on Whitchurch Common, needed an airstrip near to their base and the glider field was appropriate, considering that the field was so much larger than that at the Heath Park Cubstrip. The AOP work continued in unison with the Army based at the Heath but it is impossible to trace a battalion that was assigned to the glider field.

The Americans brought their Piper Cubs, a couple of bell tents and a weapons carrier and used the blister hangar that had been erected for the ATC's gliders to house and maintain them. The soldiers servicing the aircraft had their tents pitched along the rear of Ty-Glas Road and the hangar was at the north-east corner of the landing ground near to the tax offices. Just a few days before D-Day, 6 June 1944, the Americans left, as happened all over the UK. Today the Glider Field is only a corner of the area that it was in the war. The leisure centre, offices and warehouses cover nine tenths of it; just a small contribution but important.

As I wrote earlier, the major part of the 2nd Evacuation Unit was based on Whitchurch Common during, the period of late 1943 to June 1944. They were also living in tents on an area of Whitchurch Common, on the south side of Merthyr Road, extending to an area where the houses of Clos Cornel and Heol Coed-Cae were later to be built. The unit had its mess hall and administration on the opposite side of Merthyr Road next to Ararat Chapel.

There is a tablet on the roadside opposite the Three Elms public house, provided by the Americans in gratitude for the hospitality provided to them by the citizens of Whitchurch.

Glider Field at Llanishen. This overhead, dated the 13 May 1946, beautifully shows the large area of land available at that time. The area now has been mostly swallowed up by an industrial and commercial estate. Note that on the left of the picture half of the Royal Ordnance Factory can be seen. This has now been demolished and is a housing estate; however, the blister hangar stayed for another thirty years. (Welsh Assembly Government Photographic Archive)

The Kirby Cadet Mk l was assembled by and served with W62 Glider School at the Glider Field in Llanishen, then Pengam Moors. The glider was named Thumper and was serialed PD679. (Dr Hugh Thomas)

This photograph shows Wing Commander Guy Gibson VC of Dambuster fame visiting W62 on 4 March 1944 to encourage the lads. Gibson is standing above the car. (Dr Hugh Thomas)

The air and ground crews of the Piper Cubs used three or four tents for accommodation, a jeep, a weapons carrier and usually tended to two cubs. At the glider field they camped to the rear of homes along Ty-Glas Road, Llanishen. (Ken Wakefield)

ELEVEN

Wenvoe Airfield

ST 111741 OS

While the negotiations were going on at the City Hall over Pengam Moors in the early 1930s and occasional flying took place at Ely Racecourse, another airfield in Cardiff was in steady use at Wenvoe, situated 4 miles west of Cardiff city centre, just south of the A48 at the Tumble Hill, a few hundred yards from the pleasant hamlet of Twyn-yr-Odyn.

Cardiff Flying Club first used the field on 1 August 1931 on the undulating grassy area known as St Lythans Down, some 26 acres in area. They installed three small corrugated-steel hangars and a wooden one. A club house (a redundant railway coach), a workshop and a fuel tank were also built and were all located in the south-east corner of the field alongside the reservoir in the next field.

It was just used for club flying for a while, then other aviation interests began to look at the site as Pengam Moor was not yet complete. In January 1932 the *Bristol Evening News* attempted a regular Bristol to Cardiff cross-Channel service. Twice daily they operated with an Avro Ten (two crew and eight passengers) chartered from Imperial Airways, but it was not commercially viable and ceased after only one week.

On 10 July 1934 a licence for one year was issued to South Wales Airways Ltd. who had plans to expand the airfield. The licence was renewed a year later in 1935, but the following year they were denied. The Air Ministry inspectors said that a new licence would only be renewed if certain improvements to the actual landing surface were made, the main problem being a slight mound in the flight path, no matter which direction a pilot chose. That same mound is the very spot on which Wenvoe television mast is built. To remove this mound in those days of non-mechanisation would not have been feasible to undertake along with other projects as required by the Air Ministry.

So the years went by with private illegal landings at the site, especially when Pengam Moors was flooded. The site owner was disgusted and complained to the Air Ministry, stating that a fully laden Armstrong Whitworth Argosy and three RAF Hawker Audax carrying senior RAF Officers had used the airfield with the argument 'What's good enough for the RAF should be good enough for other flyers, so licence me!'

Then in December 1938 the Straight Corporation applied for a temporary licence to use Wenvoe as the terminal for the cross-Channel (Bristol) scheduled service whenever Pengam Moors was unusable.

They were granted a one month's licence on 23 December with the proviso that rescue equipment and a wind sock were installed and were renewed several times during the early part of 1939. Use of Wenvoe was restricted to DH 84 Dragon aircraft in low wind conditions.

The area of St Lythans Down up high on a plateau. The aerodrome (as it was then called) is dotted to show the extent of the landing area. Dated 4 December 1946, it is about twenty years before the BBC decided to build their television mast on the site. (Welsh Assembly Government Photographic Archive)

On 1 February South Wales Airways objected to the licence being issued to the Straight Corporation and the Air Ministry said there was no question of a permanent licence being issued to anybody.

In March the Cardiff Aeroplane Club, also victims of Pengam Moors' waterlogged surface, asked the Air Ministry for permission to use Wenvoe for circuits and bumps but no response was ever recorded. The last temporary licence was issued in June 1939, by which time Pengam Moors was fully serviceable and Wenvoe passed into history.

The runways were, from north to south, a maximum length of 1,500ft and east to west 1,350ft.

Mr Bill Greatrex, who is now in his late seventies, helped me to view the airfield. Except for the television mast, the fields are much as they were when he was a lad in the 1930s. He recalls 'Alan Cobham's Air Display' on the field and also tells me that

The western end of the aerodrome site; the base of the mast is in roughly the place where the rise in the ground prevented flying here. (Ivor Jones)

This is the Avro Ten that flew from Wenvoe in the attempt to forge a new air service from Cardiff. (A.V. Roe Ltd)

Cardiff Aero Club used Wenvoe whenever Pengam Moors was flooded or muddy. (Mervyn Amundsen)

because he lived so close to the airfield, when he heard the sound of approaching aircraft, he would run into the field to disperse the sheep. All the pilots would kindly do a big circuit to give him time. He was sometimes rewarded by an air trip for the small price of 2s 6d. He said that this was affordable to him because he had the Wenvoe newspaper round each day.

TWELVE

Wenvoe Camp Airstrip

Grid Reference ST 124706, Barry, South Glamorgan

This army camp was built on land that was part of the large estate, including Wenvoe Castle and the golf club of that name, in 1940.

The land at this part of the estate was undulating and it must have been difficult to site the huts and tents that filled the field, but the flatter area to the west of the camp was suitable for use by the Air Observation Post L4 Piper Cubs that accompanied the artillery battalions of the US Army accommodated here at various periods in 1943 and 1944.

The camp had served British Army units and their allies before the Americans came, and after they had no further need of Wenvoe it was put to further use as a prisoner of war camp for Germans, and later Italians.

The airstrip runs alongside Port Road East (A4050) and approximately from the camp's entrance road westward to the only houses that existed at the time, about 500 yards away, and it was the southern side of a square field.

The first of the artillery units to arrive was the 115th Field Artillery Battalion USArmy in March 1944. This is believed to have been a unit of the 90th Division, VII Corps Army. When this unit left Wenvoe to go to the embarkation ports for D-Day on 6 June, it was replaced by the 38th Field Artillery Battalion of the 2nd Division V Corps. From 16 May to 2/3 June they were to embark as follow-up troops.

Today there is no sign of what was once home for thousands of men of different nationalities. In the camp area the grass and brambles are 4 or 5ft high and it is difficult to look for concrete hut bases. There was a concrete parade square there at one time. All that is to be seen, down in the valley, is a golf driving range.

The entrance gate leading to Wenvoe Camp as it is today. (Ivor Jones)

Wenvoe Army Camp, June 1960. Much of the camp has been removed and only the concrete bases remain. The airstrip is to the left. (Welsh Assembly Government Photographic Archive)

The landing ground at the camp looking north in 2005. (Ivor Jones)

THIRTEEN

The Barry Golf Club and Highlight Farm Camp and Airstrip

Grid Reference ST 104695

The camp was originally built for the British Army, just as the camp at Wenvoe – a mile or so to the east, but both were to accommodate US troops as the war progressed. There was also a large anti-aircraft site (UK) on this area of land just a few yards to the west of the camp which, while under the British occupation, was known as Highlight Farm Camp, after the farm to the north of it. The access to the farm was Highlight Lane that ran from Port Road, through the camp to the farm properties.

When the Americans arrived in 1942 (this is the date that the history of the golf club advises) they needed more space. They did what the British would never have dared to do – they took over the area of land in front of the first tee and the eighteenth hole fairway to erect a tented camp, as well as the existing former British area. They now named the place Barry Golf Club Camp. Although the name of the club was actually Brynhill Golf Club this was probably to give an indication of the geographical location of the camp to the army.

The preparations for the landings in Europe included a decision to base US troops in the west of the UK, the British and Canadians to the east, and this stance was to be maintained during the landings: US to the west, UK to the east.

The follow-up troops of the Americans were lodged in southern Wales and it was difficult to find barracks for these men who were not only passing through but trying to get some tactical exercises in, ready for the battle to come.

In December 1943 one of the units to arrive here at Barry was the 115th Field Artillery Battalion of the 1st Army, which was not tied to any particular division (an independent FA Battalion). They were to stay for a fairly long spell at the camp – some up to six months.

They had a happy time with the people of Barry and long relationships were forged. Perhaps the soldiers' feelings were of relief after leaving their previous posting – Iceland.

Because of overcrowding perhaps, one battery of this battalion was transferred elsewhere, possibly to Heath Camp, Cardiff. They trained at Crow Hill training area near Wenvoe, and probably trained at landing craft embarkation and disembarkation at one of the beaches nearby, such as Penarth.

16 May 1944 saw the arrival of another FA Battalion, the 15th of the 2nd Infantry Division, who moved in from nearby Porthcawl, where they had spent a month. But now they were to train, and combine, with the 9th Infantry Regiment to form a

Barry Golf Club was the name given by US Army documents for what is Brynhill Golf Club. Dated 3 June 1950, today little remains. Some of the huts are intact and some of the concrete bases can be seen. The tents occupied many fields, even onto the course itself in the run up to D-Day. It is believed that the cubstrip was across the road from the camp, where there is now a school and its sports field. (Welsh Assembly Government Photographic Archive)

The cubstrip from the north-east. The sports field and buildings with the trees were not there sixty years ago. The camp was to the right and across Port Road. (Ivor Jones)

The cubstrip from the south-west. The army camp was across the road to the left. (Ivor Jones)

Combat Team, which was the latest idea for success in the invasion. This was happening to most infantry, and artillery units. No doubt the necessary spell at Sennybridge Ranges was part of this.

The Combat Team left Barry Golf Course on 2/3 June 1944, and boarded the US Army Transport 'George Goethals' in Swansea docks, then sailed on 7 June to land on 'Omaha Easy Red' beach, Normandy.

My search to find the airstrip serving this camp is still unfinished. The wartime captain of the golf club and also its leading historian today insist that they did not fly from any part of the golf course; in fact the flattest area was covered in huts and tents through 1944.

I have corresponded with the son of a sergeant of the 115th FA Battalion who served here and flew the L4 AOPs until promotion made him captain and Headquarters Battery Commander. It was non-commisioned officers who piloted the AOPs. His son, who himself is a retired major in the US Army serving in Korea and Vietnam, states that his father – now deceased – talked little of his experiences in the war but he did talk of the fine time that they had at Barry. But it seems that the field was used by two battalions, which means four Cubs would have to be nearby and I have opted, until someone can tell me differently, for the field lying across the Port Road to the main entrance to the camp, which is now the sports field for Barry Comprehensive School. With the lack of people of the age to know what occurred here sixty years ago, and the American method of dealing with local government, nothing is written down.

When the US Army left for France all these units had their tents gathered up, leaving the huts and permanent buildings on site. These were immediately put to use for housing POWs – Germans and Italians – where they stayed for quite a long time working on farms and civil projects. The whole site is now housing but on the golf course one hut remains. On the old Ack Ack site of the British artillery is the store and car park of Tesco.

This is the only remnant of the American occupation at Brynhill. Once a supply store, it is now used to house the clubs, lawn mowers and other equipment. (Ivor Jones)

FOURTEEN

RAF Rhoose/Cardiff International Airport

Grid Reference ST 064674, 3 miles west of Barry, South Glamorgan, near B4265/A4226

When RAF Llandow opened as an ASU (Aircraft Storage Unit) on 1 April 1940, it was called upon also to host a training unit. This was happening to other storage and Maintenance Units as the need to evacuate these schools to areas away from intervention from the Luftwaffe was urgent. Not only to allow the trainee pilots to apply their attention exclusively to their work, but also to free up airfields in the south-east to operational squadrons.

In Llandow's case the outfit they were allocated was No.53 Operational Training Unit and, as in most cases, this meant that a satellite airfield was necessary nearby to share the workload on Llandow's facilities. That was why Rhoose was built.

The site of this airfield was a few hundred yards from the sea to the south at Rhoose village, and to the north the village of Penmark. It was completed and opened on 7 April 1942 to the relief of all at Llandow.

The arrival of B Flight of No.53 OTU at Llandow on 24 June 1941 had left A&C flights at Heston where they were to form No.61 OTU. With B Flight flown in, the HQ and the main party arrived on 1 July 1941, with twenty-seven (plus nine in reserve) MkI Spitfires, ten (plus four) Masters, and three Target Towers, all under the control of No.81 Group.

The trainees used Rhoose from its opening as the runways were busy at Llandow, but there was little hangarage or accommodation at the satellite so, of course, the maintenance of the aircraft was still done at the parent base.

The British, Canadian, Australian and New Zealander pilots, hundreds of them, did their combat training and dogfighting in the skies of Glamorgan for the two years of the unit's tenancy of Rhoose. Many of these lads were killed or were badly injured in this deadly game.

By 1943 it was clear that the airfield at Rhoose was poorly laid out and was responsible for many accidents, and injuries. Planning was afoot to relieve some of the growing congestion caused by the cruciform pattern of the runways, caused by the continuous take offs and landings, as the establishment of the unit was now fifty-six (plus nineteen in reserve) Spitfires, seventeen (plus five) Masters and four (plus two) Target Towers, Defiants, then later the Martinets.

Mr Hugh Trivett has provided me with some facts on the casualties of No.53 OTU shared between Llandow and Rhoose. At least ninety-two Spitfires were lost, fifty were

The station started with its runways in a simple cross – two concrete runways
meeting at their centres. It was a recipe for trouble and after a short time of service
it was changed to the form shown in this overhead of 1944. It was to stay like
this until the post-war large, fast airliners needed a longer run, and this runway
(seen running from the top left-hand corner to the right-hand side of picture) was
adopted for lengthening to form a single runway. The village of Rhoose is in the
foreground. (Welsh Assembly Government Photographic Archive)

written off (Cat. E), fourteen damaged but repairable (Cat. B) and about eight ended
up in the sea. The fate of the remainder is unknown, as the records at the Air Historical
Branch of the MOD went missing many years ago.

The majority of the spitfires used at the OTU were war weary and worn, before
joining the unit.

The Spitfire Mk II is of No.53 Operational Training Unit at RAF Rhoose, which was the satellite station to RAF Llandow. (Frank Jones)

Large numbers of these Miles Master IIs were with No.53 OTU and were based at Rhoose for pilot training. (John Hamlin)

Rhoose in the spring of 1942. No.53 OTU pilots and instructors outside the debriefing control van. The pilot with his hands on his hips is Ted Bristow. These men were mostly sergeants – don't they look young? But how many survived the war? (Phillip Davies)

This Robin hangar is still in position, and is used by the Aero Club. It is one of few RAF buildings left here. (Ivor Jones)

The spitfires on service here regularly:

1 Crashed into the mountains north of the airfield, some of which rise to 2000 feet.
2 Collided with other aircraft, both in the air and on take-off and landing.
3 Stalled and span in.

Examples: 7 July 1941, Spitfires X4024 and X 4607 collided during a training session. X4024 crashed on a house in Mount Pleasant, Merthyr, killing several people and the Canadian pilot Sgt G.F. Manuel. X4607 crashed in a field between Mount Pleasant and Quackers Yard, killing the pilot, Sgt L. Goldberry of the RCAF. Both of these aircraft had flown in the Battle of Britain with No.92 Squadron.

On 9 July 1941 Spitfire N3230 crashed and burned out. This had flown in the Battle of Britain with No.64 Squadron. Also on 9 July, Spitfire P9383 crashed and burned out at the village of Colwinston, killing the pilot Sgt F.G.T. McGahy. This aircraft also flew in the Battle of Britain with No.616 Squadron.

On 10 July 1941, Spitfire X4988, during dog-fighting practice, attempted an upward roll, fell into a spin, recovered and flicked into another spin and crashed at Marcross Aerodrome at 3.30 p.m. The pilot, M.A. Plomteau, RCAF, is buried at Llantwit Major.

On 6 August 1941 Spitfire X4381 was on a general training flight when the starboard wing broke away during a dive. The aircraft, a former Battle of Britain Spitfire that had flown with No.152 Squadron, crashed into a hill near Ton Pentre killing the pilot, Flt Lt M.A. Goodwin.

On 12 August 1941 Spitfire R7057 came out of cloud and flew at 1,960ft into Graig-y-Llyn, Pen-y-Cae, above Rhigos, at 7 p.m. killing the pilot, Plt Off. C.J. Day, RAFVR.

26 August 1941 saw Spitfire X4263 crash at Rhoose Point at 1.15 p.m., killing the pilot, Sgt J.P. MacIlwane. This was another Battle of Britain Spitfire, with No.603 Squadron.

On 11 September 1941 Spitfire K9976 stalled and spun in, after entering a steep dive, and crashed near St Mary's Church, Flemingstone, killing the pilot Sgt R.E. Murray, RCAF.

Also on the 11th, Spitfire K9930 was abandoned by its pilot, Sgt Cresswell, due to a jammed aileron and it crashed near Lake Farm, Cowbridge. The pilot was unhurt. The plane was ex-Battle of Britain, flown with No.152 Squadron.

On 15 September 1941 Spitfire N3198 force landed and crashed at Llandow and was struck off charge.

On 25 September 1941 Spitfire L1054 dived into the sea half a mile south-east of Llantwit Major killing the pilot Sgt G.F. Parker.

These are just a few of the OTU's early disasters but the carnage continued until No.53 OTU's days in Wales ceased when the whole unit was transferred to Kirton-in-Lindsay on 9 May 1943.

The airfield at Rhoose lay quiet for ten months, then the place was made ready, in something of an emergency, for the intake of another unit.

No.7 Air Gunnery School
This Unit had been based at Stormy Down since the war began, but the poor airfield surface had caused many accidents and extensive repairs, drainage and the building of a hard runway was needed there. While this was being done No.7 Gunnery School

A Martinet of No.7 Air Gunnery School which had moved from Stormy Down to Rhoose from where No.53 OTU had just left.

Anson of No.7 AGS at Rhoose, flying over the Bristol Channel. Note the towed drogue above the gunner firing from the turret. (Frank Jones)

was moved temporarily to Rhoose. On Tuesday 8 February 1944 twenty-three Ansons, twenty Martinets and fifty pilots moved 10 miles or so eastward to continue their drogue towing and firing along the same coastlines as before.

Target tugs of No.587 Squadron, which was an anti-aircraft co-operation unit, were also using Rhoose on detachment at the time and it was somewhat busy on the airfield. Orders were therefore issued that all No.7 AG aircraft were to have airmen at the wing tips when taxiing to prevent collisions.

There was a change to establishment on 27 April 1944. Six Ansons were added, making twenty-seven for use and ten in reserve, plus two dual-control machines. Martinets were reduced by seven to total eighteen, with ten in reserve. On 1 May three Ansons arrived from No.9 (O) AFU Penrhos to complete the strength.

Rhoose is now Cardiff
Airport and this 1950s
photograph shows a
BEA Dakota about
to leave. Note the
original Control Tower/
Watch Office (Drng
No.4805/41). (Mervyn
Amundsen)

On 4 May Sgt E. Janiszewski (Polish) in Martinet JN420 ran out of fuel on his
approach to drop a sleeve on Rhoose. He force landed safely on the airfield.

7 May saw Martinet MS836 of No.587 Squadron in trouble. The engine cut out on
take-off. The aircraft ran through the perimeter fence, into a field, and turned over. The
crew were unhurt.

Four days later No.587 Squadron aircraft, attached for target duties on Thornbury
Maritime Royal Artillery School range, returned to Cardiff (Pengam Moors).

Monday 8 May was a black day for No.7 AGS with eight deaths. Three Ansons took off
from Rhoose on cinegun exercise with a Martinet. Ansons LV300 and MG131 collided
about 1½ miles out at sea from Porthcawl Point. The duty boat put to sea but found
only an empty dinghy and some wreckage. Eventually all the bodies were found and
buried at Nottage.

The month of June began with a taxiing accident when Flt Sgt Foes, in Martinet
JN419, hit an open door on a petrol bowser. On the 18th the same sergeant took off in
Martinet MS675, with L.A.C. Stover as target operator. His engine seized at 1,500ft and
he made a good landing at Rhoose. Swinging to avoid parked aircraft he hit a picket
block and the undercart collapsed.

Suddenly news arrived that because of the reduction in training requirements, the air
gunner schools were to be reorganised. No.7 AGS was to disband by 2 September 1944
and No.8 AGS at Evanton by 28 August.

Other units affected were No.1 at Pembrey, No.2 at Dalcross and No.3 at Castle
Kennedy, which were to have pupil capacities of 360 each. No.4 AGS Morpeth and
No.11 AGS at Andreas were to have 240 each. Capacity at No.10 AGS Barrow was to be
240 WOP/AG. At Bishops Court No.12 AGS would have 160 flight engineer and flight
mechanic trainees. No.9 (O) AFU was to hold up to 120 air gunners.

On 2 August all aircraft returned from Rhoose to Stormy Down, where the
runways had still not been laid, as the need for the rest of the war did not warrant
it, and preparations were made to close Rhoose down. It was transferred to No.40
Group, Maintenance Command, on 1 November, becoming a sub-site of No.214 MU
at Newport's Docks. This was a little known Maintenance Unit and was responsible
for most of the shipments and stockholding for the RAF. As a sub site it was used for
storage. When No.59 MU formed at Newland, Gloucestershire, it absorbed Rhoose
as a detached site for the explosives storage unit from 6 June 1945. On 15 April 1946

the whole unit moved to Rhoose from Newland, but only to disband in February 1947.

Strangely, the airfield had reached its best configuration at the end of No.7 AGS's tenure. The runways had comprised a simple cross at middle of the field, but now the extension to the north-east to south-west runway from 1,100 yards to 1,560 yards, and the improved peri-track associated with it, enabled aircraft to move without impeding others. The other runway 13/31 south-east to north-west received no extension at this time, but in years to come would be developed into the main runway for Cardiff International Airport. There had never been any excess maintenance hangars here, just four enlarged over blister hangars on the northern hardstands.

A small watch office/control tower of brick (Drng No.4885/41) was positioned inside the southern peri-track, adjacent to the south-east to north-west runway 13/31.

Rhoose had by now built up a fair showing of domestic sites; the usual airmen's, sergeants', and officers' sleeping sites were on one side of the road and the WAAF's well away on the other. There was also a communal site, sick quarters and the usual messes.

While No.53 OTU was here their aircraft were serviced at Llandow. When No.7 AGS occupied the airfield, servicing of their aircraft was carried out at Stormy Down.

With the disbanding of the bomb store of No.59 MU and the sub-site of No.214 MU, the airfield closed in approximately January 1948 and the place lay dormant for four years.

In the early fifties the Irish State Airline, Aer Lingus, had been trying hard to set up a route between Dublin and Cardiff, when Cardiff's Municipal Airport was still at Pengam Moors. This was not an airport that could handle the Aer Lingus DC3s, and anyway at that time there was much discussion on the future of Pengam as planning permission was about to be passed allowing the building of a mini steel works right in the runway's path.

Special arrangements were made for Aer Lingus to use Rhoose. Ground staff were switched to Rhoose for each individual movement, starting in 1952. The Ministry of Transport and Civil Aviation (MTCA) were drawn in and by 1954 all operations, including those of Cambrian Airways had been transferred to Rhoose.

Conditions were primitive. The RAF base had been allowed to become almost derelict and there was no sanitation. The MTCA spent £30,000 on strengthening and resurfacing the runways, the wartime buildings were converted into terminal buildings and a T2 hangar was brought from Withybush Airfield (Haverfordwest) at a cost of £100,000.

In June 1952 the first service by Aer Lingus from Dublin to Rhoose was inaugurated with a DC3 and, by the end of the first year of operations, carried nearly 6,000 passengers between the two cities. In 1969 (ending in March) 15,000 passengers, and 108,000kg of freight were carried between Ireland and South Wales alone. In fact, at that time, it was the best route to America from the South Wales area. Daily flights linked Cardiff to Dublin and the company's Boeing Jet network from Dublin to New York, Boston, Chicago, and Montreal.

The company introduced BAC 1-11s and Boeing 737s on the Cardiff to Dublin route in 1970, but inexplicably dropped the route in the mid-1970s. This route was snapped up by Manx Airlines and Ryanair who both still operate from Cardiff. Manx was incorporated into British Regional Airways.

When Cambrian Air Services was forced to leave Pengam Moors Airport, they joined Aer Lingus at Rhoose two years later in 1954, and flying the DC3s they flourished.

Cambrian Air Service's Dakotas at Rhoose. They are at the old terminal on the south side of the airfield. (Ken Wakefield)

Cambrian brought this T2 hangar from Withybush (Haverfordwest) Airfield to provide a maintenance base for their fleet. The modification to the upper doorway was to accommodate the Viscount and its tail fin. This hangar was pronounced unsafe and demolished in around 2000. (Ivor Jones)

The company sold off its five Rapides and, with the two Dakotas brought from Staverton, started work. Using Dakotas meant the airline now had to have stewardesses for the first time, just two for now, but eventually a total of fourteen girls to cover flights to Paris, the Channel Islands, Cork, Manchester and Glasgow.

On 23 May 1955 CAS was renamed Cambrian Airways and a company DH Dove No.G-AKSK crashed at Fritham, killing the pilot Bob Carson. The plane was on a flight from Cardiff to Southampton and then Paris and there were six passengers on board. Luckily the pilot was the only fatality.

Above: A Cambrian Dakota climbing after take-off. (Ken Wakefield)

Right: Glamorgan Aero Club, flying school and private aircraft take up space on the ramps at Rhoose. (Ivor Jones)

This was a move up from the Dakota – the DH Heron of Cambrian Airways. (Ken Wakefield)

Viscounts on the ramp of Cambrian Airways at Cardiff/Rhoose Airport. (Ken Wakefield)

A new route to Nice from Cardiff and Bristol was started, but was not financially viable, and was dropped.

In November an order was placed for two DH Herons. The order was increased to three later. These aircraft came into service in the spring of 1956, Registration Nos G-AOGO; G-AORJ and G-AOGU.

Cambrian was now becoming a big airline, and this was recognised by BEA who entered into a ten-year agreement with Cambrian, giving the Welsh airline the traffic rights from Liverpool to the Channel Islands, and from Manchester to Jersey, via Cardiff and Bristol.

In 1957 Bristol also received a new airport at Lulsgate, so Cambrian moved from Whitchurch, over to Lulsgate.

Cambrian also began operating from Fairwood Common, which had been opened as Swansea Airport on 1 June 1956. The first flight was Heron G-AORJ for Jersey.

In 1958 BEA acquired a one-third interest in Cambrian and at the board meeting they decided on a 15 per cent increase in operations for the future of Wales and the West of England's services, but this didn't work, because 1958 saw a dramatic downturn, and recession in travel business, so bad that Cambrian was forced to sell off its aircraft, and make many of its staff redundant. They retained just one Rapide for the Manchester–Cardiff–Bristol run. The company reported a loss of £102,380 for the year ending 31 December 1958.

1959 saw an improvement and a new chairman, Mr John Morgan, who brought more energy into the company. At the same time, Wing Commander Bill Elwin became MD and BEA came to the aid of Cambrian. The state airline leased to the company three Pionairs, Registration Nos G-AHCZ, G-AGIP and G-ALXL, at the cheap rate of £7 per flying hour. On 2 March scheduled services were resumed from Liverpool to Jersey, via Cardiff and Bristol, and from Cardiff and Bristol, to Southampton and Paris.

At the end of the year, the Pionairs were purchased by Cambrian from BEA and, in addition, two more were bought later: registration nos G–AMEV and G–AMJX, making a fleet of five.

On 1 April 1960, Cambrian inaugurated the service to Belfast, cancelled in the crisis of 1958, together with all the other destinations forfeited at that time.

In 1961 three more Pionairs were acquired from BEA and with a new airport having been opened in Cork, Cambrian introduced services there from London, Bristol and Cardiff. By the end of September they had increased its traffic by 34 per cent over the same period the year before (52,585 in 1960 and 70,632 in 1961).

In 1962, the company established their own engineering base, to do the maintenance work previously done by BEA. Cardiff and Bristol to Glasgow commenced on 1 April 1962.

1963 saw BEA giving more routes to Cambrian that they themselves had found loss-making. They were linking flights, Isle of Man with Belfast, Liverpool, Manchester and London. These routes now made Cambrian the second largest independent operator in the UK and to enable them to operate these routes, BEA sold them five Viscounts together with a lot of spares for the price of £750,000. 1962 saw Cambrian carry 1,777,341 passengers.

In 1963 the airline started new routes to Nice, Rimini and Valencia in cooperation with 'Hourmonts', the local travel agent. In 1963 Cambrian numbered seventy-six engineers, thirty-six pilots and twenty-eight cabin staff. Following the acquisition of Viscounts, the Pionair's fleet was reduced to five, G–AGIP, G– AMJX, and G–AMFV being sold. This last one found its way to Gibraltar Airways, with whom it flew the shuttle to Tangier, logging 10,558 crossings, before replacement on 30 March 1970. The two Dakotas were sold.

In 1965 three more Viscounts were bought, making the fleet of eight in number, but G–AMOL, carrying freight only, crashed at Speke Airport. The runways were still not long enough for modern jets and the company could not compete with the likes of Luton or Gatwick.

1966 saw the purchase of five more Viscounts from Channel Airways at a cost of £750,000. The first six months of the year was a record period for Cambrian, with 350,000 passengers on scheduled services (35 per cent more).

1967 saw Cambrian needing more capital and it turned to BEA for help. But help was also needed by another independent airline, BKS from the north-east of England, who were in the same boat as Cambrian. British European Airways needed both companies to service and serve their local communities so they encouraged the two to merge but retain their own identities.

1968 saw the last Dakota flights from Paris to Rhoose to be sold. The Viscount fleet was now twelve strong and Pionairs numbered five. This year also saw the departure of Wg Cdr Bill Elwin. He resigned as managing director in March after eighteen years with the company because he could see that Cambrian was losing its identity as the only truly Welsh airline. His job was shared by Mr Jim Callan and Mr David Davies becoming joint general managers.

Captain de Wilde retired after eighteen years' service. When he had joined in 1950 the airline had three pilots; now, on his leaving, 153 were employed. 31 October saw the last flights of the Pionairs. These were retired and Cambrian became a fleet of eleven Viscounts.

In 1968 one of Cambrian's rivals – British Eagle – collapsed and within twelve hours Cambrian took over their operation of Liverpool to Glasgow and Liverpool to London routes. It was a tough world for the independent companies.

Cardiff International Airport in 1980. (Welsh Assembly Government Photographic Archive)

1969 saw the engineering base at Rhoose become the maintenance base for all British Air Services (BAS). This was then named Airways Engineering. BAS was the title of the group formed by British European Airways to keep BKS and Cambrian alive. BEA did not want the routes served by the independents, as they knew that they would be unprofitable, so it was in their best interest to encourage them. A holding company was formed, British Air Services, which was 70 per cent owned by BEA. BAS then acquired 100 per cent interest in both Cambrian and BKS, which was renamed North-Eastern Airlines. In December the first of Cambrian's BAC 1-11s was obtained from Autair.

The BKS side of the partnership was losing money fast so in an attempt to stem the flow Jim Callan was sent from Rhoose, after twenty years' service, to Hounslow to work for BKS. The new sole managing director at Rhoose was David Davies.

In a very eventful year at this growing airport, 1970 saw the long-awaited extension to what was to be the main runway (13/31) to a length of 7,000ft for the introduction of jets. The Barry to Llantwit Major road had to be diverted to miss the southern extension of the runway. The work cost £5 million and was to be ready for the international rugby match Ireland *v.* Wales, when Cambrian and Aer Lingus used Viscounts, BAC 1-11s and Boeing 737s put on 168 extra flights to carry approximately 7,000 Welsh supporters to Dublin.

Other users of this runway were the Comets of Dan-Air that were used for holiday charters: Court Lines with BAC 1-11s and British Midlands using Viscounts and Heralds. To go with the new runway a new technical block and a fine control tower at the north-east boundary were built. In November 1969, Cambrian began a service between

This is a BAC 1-11 of Cambrian Airways just outside the terminal building at Cardiff Wales Airport in 1970. (Ken Wakefield)

Cardiff and London, providing a link between South Wales and the rest of the world, but 1969 saw the end of some other routes. In September the service from Swansea to Dublin and Jersey was withdrawn and in the same month the Cardiff to Dinard service came to an end.

The company had bought its first BAC 1-11 in December 1969. Five more were bought of which were registration nos G-AVOE, G-AVOF and G-AVGP. Cambrian had a new chairman, Mr George T. Cantlay, and they decided to go into holiday charter business. The company was named Cambrian Holidays and took up agreements with the holiday agents Hourmont. Trips to Arenal, Benidorm and Torremolinos became frequent. On 1 April Cambrian began a service to Dubrovnic in Croatia (then Yugoslavia) which was formerly a BEA route.

Operationally Cambrian was split into two fleets (on three bases) and Capt. Ken Wakefield was made fleet captain of the BAC 1-11s and Capt. Ash Goodhew fleet captain of the Viscounts (Liverpool-based).

1973 saw the start of a service to Lyon five times weekly with BAC 1-11s. Significantly, in 1974 BEA and BOAC, which also included BAS, merged so now Cambrian became an integral part of British Airways, as the new state airline was called. On 1 April the name of Cambrian finally disappeared, when the company's staff, planes and equipment were absorbed into British Airways, as it could not survive without state help. Despite its cash problems it was a successful company, flying the flag of Wales for forty years.

BAS merged into BEA Birmingham and BEA Jersey to become British Regional Airways Division shortly after operations ceased in 1978.

British Airways pulled out of Cardiff, at least as far as scheduled services were concerned, on 1 April 1980. British Regional had gradually built up a feeder service in and out of Cardiff.

On the departure of Cambrian, the engineering base at Cardiff was used by the parent, until they too left. These facilities at the old Cambrian base were taken over by British Air Ferries, where they designed and built an aircraft, a two-seat micro-light. The prototype, G-MMAA, first flew on 8 July 1982 and they were to sell for £4,000. British Air Ferries suffered many set backs and when new management took over they not only abandoned the aircraft but the engineering base as well.

British Airways' Viscount at Cardiff Wales Airport in the late 1970s. (Mervyn Amundsen)

Cardiff International Airport's single runway configuration on 18 June 1986. (Welsh Assembly Government Photographic Archive)

The new Air Traffic Control building at Cardiff International Airport – airside view. (Ivor Jones)

Norman Aeroplane Co. (the result of a split in the famous Britten-Norman Co.) moved into Rhoose to a fine new hangar-workshop behind the old T2 hangar in 1986.

NAC were to produce crop dusters and water bombers under the guise of the Fieldmaster, a fine trainer in the Firecracker and a four-seat tourer named Freelance. They were all good designs, but the competition ensured that the NAC failed shortly after they began serious production and vacated the site by 1990.

There were many other companies plying their services from Cardiff, including Dan-Air which operated from Rhoose from the late 1950s through to the mid-1970s, running the Cardiff to Liverpool and Newcastle route. They also began flights to Norway, Holland, Belgium, and the Isle of Man. They struggled and, like many other smaller airlines, vanished from the regional airports.

The 1970s saw the holiday flying boom with the advent of the Court Line, coupled with the local travel agency Hourmont. Clarksons, the brightly painted BAC 1-11s, were to be seen regularly at Rhoose until this company crashed too.

Brittania Airways continues to operate as it has done since the 1960s taking holiday makers to places like Spain, Canaries, Greece and Turkey. Airtours have also had a large and continuing interest in Cardiff since the company was formed.

Channel Airways was a regular operator from Rhoose, mostly charter and all-inclusive tour flights. When the Glamorgan triumvirate decided to sell Rhoose, it became the property of the investment company TBI and they named their airport Cardiff International. This is the last of an interminable list of names this place has endured since its opening in the 1950s. When the Ministry of Transport and Civil Aviation ran it, it was merely Rhoose Airport. In 1965 it was acquired by Glamorgan County Council who reasonably named it Glamorgan (Rhoose) Airport. Then, in 1978, it became Cardiff (Wales).

It is international in so far as KLM do five flights daily to Amsterdam. British Regional Airways operate from Cardiff to Belfast, Edinburgh, Glasgow and Aberdeen. To the Continent they fly to Paris, Brussels, and Guernsey. Manx – in the form of British Regional Airways – offer twice daily flights to Jersey from here.

Concorde at Cardiff on one of its excursions from here in 1990. (Ivor Jones)

From April 2000, the air fleet of Air 2000 has operated a base at Cardiff, with a staff of seventy and use of the full cabin staff and aircrew facilities at the excellent St David's Hotel at Cardiff Bay.

Monarch, Air Europa, Brittania, Spanair, Cypress Airways, all the usual carriers one would expect at a mid-size airport are to be seen, though it is fair to say that there are more aircraft movements by night than by day.

A weekly Boeing 747 flight to Orlando, Florida, operated by Airtours has been established here.

TBI, who own Cardiff International, also bought Belfast Airport in 1996, Orlando (Sanford) in 1997 and Skavsta (Sweden) in 1998, and are currently looking for the council's approval for expansion in the Business Park outside the airfield here. The chairman of the company is a local man and the latest acquisition, I understand, is Prestwick Airport.

One of the latest operators to work from Cardiff is Direct Holidays. With a £10 million investment here, they intend to do a lot of business from Cardiff, and have commenced with 200 sun seekers to Salou. From April 2000 they would use destinations that include Spain, the Canaries and Greece and had a 43 per cent increase for the year 2001. The management of Cardiff International is pleased with Direct Holidays' plans for the future as it will take Cardiff's capacity to over 1.5 million passengers, an increase of 21 per cent on the summer of 1999.

Direct Holidays intend to run a busy winter schedule, as well as an expanding summer programme in competition with Thomson, Airtours, First Choice, JMC and Cosmos. Air Wales (Awyr Cymru), a new company with expansion in mind, operates two Dornier 228s, leased from Islanflug in Iceland. Swansea and Cardiff International are its bases, with flights to Stansted, Cork, Dublin three times a week, and more destinations are planned.

The biggest news for this airport was the arrival of BMI Baby, which began its cut price travel to popular destinations from Cardiff in October 2002. Cardiff is to be the

The vast hangar that was built by British Airways to maintain their fleet of Boeing 747s and 777s at Cardiff International Airport. (British Airways)

second base for the company and it seems to be a very successful idea. With flights to Cork, Munich, Palma, Geneva, Milan, Faro, Alicante and Malaga, they will operate forty international flights a week.

The evolution of the airfield itself was a gradual process. Before 1970 the main runway was the north-east to south-west 03/21 which had been extended in the improvements of 1944 to 4,534ft long. However, it was impractical to extend further for the modern heavy jets coming into use but the other subsidiary runway was. This was the north-west–south-east 13/31 runway. It had been extended from 3,000ft to 3,700ft since its RAF days and it could be lengthened further to 7,000ft. Taking their combined ownership very seriously, the county councils decided on the extensions to the runway at 7,000ft. Taxi-ways were completed and a new terminal was built on the opposite side of the airfield to the one used by the RAF, and Cambrian used the annexe running along the side of the T2 hangar. With the terminal came a new air traffic control tower and meteorological office. This cost the three authorities £5 million.

The new meteorological office was installed in an ideal exposed site in the north-west corner of the field, with the instrument enclosure adjacent. This office was at Llandow Airfield until 1954, transferring to the old RAF site at Rhoose in April of 1954. It not only provides advice to the flying aspect of the area, but also the general public of Wales with its forecasts.

Rhoose is 67m above mean sea level and is 1,500m inland from the Bristol Channel, with the Welsh mountains rising from about 15 kilometres to the north.

On the old RAF site to the south of the main runway is the aero-club's Cardiff Flying Club, Flying School and Helicopter School run by Heli-Air Ltd. The old T2 hangar that had been bought from Witheybush houses the privately owned planes and those of the clubs. The T2 has, at some time beyond the memory of anyone employed here now, had its original door gantries replaced with the those of a Callender Hamilton. In early

2002, this old hangar was found to be dangerously corroded and was condemned. It was demolished a few months later.

The original control tower was demolished by 1980. The main runway was extended to 7,723ft in 1982. The other is not in use.

The British Airways Maintenance Hangar at Cardiff

I was fortunate to be invited to an employees' family open day at this fine establishment in October 2000. It is sited at the northern end of Cardiff International Airport. This hangar is devoted to the repair and service of BA's considerable fleet of Boeing 747 and 777 aircraft.

The hangar has three bays, two of which are dedicated to 747s and the third which can accommodate either the 747 or 777. The system of berthing these giants involves the towing into a pre-positioned mark so that the nose of the aircraft is introduced into a shaped slot in the second floor of the hangar. This is named the mezzanine floor and it extends the full length of the building, with an area of 6,000 square metres. It has the width of a wide road, extending from the back wall of the hangar to the leading edge of the aircraft at its root. The level of this floor is just beneath the cabin doors when the plane is supported on its supports with the centre-line level.

When the scaffolds and walkways have enclosed the length of the fuselage and both wings are also surrounded by scaffolds, the huge structure that envelopes the tail assembly is swung around, from left and right, with the work staging to allow every foot of the tall vertical stabiliser to be examined.

The ground floor has the pits for the retraction of the massive undercarriages; the engines are worked on at this level, and the engine pylons, which does provide a regular chore. The underside of the wings and fuselage are, of course, worked on from the ground; the wings have their own workways. Well off the ground, but safe on rigid scaffolds that slope with the dihedral of the wing, work on ailerons and flaps can be carried out.

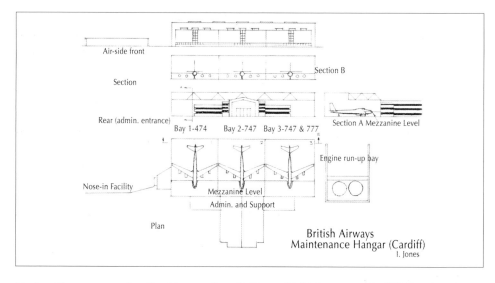

My humble attempt to describe this marvellous facility at BA Maintenance, Cardiff. (Ivor Jones)

Showing the main
undercarriage of the Boeing
777 undergoing test at the pit
at this fine working hangar.
(Ivor Jones)

This impressive place was opened by The Prince of Wales in June 1993, but the work had already begun in the February. There are 800 employees and approximately 100 contractors on site on a permanent basis. These are the systems specialists and technicians.

The front of the hangar has a large apron that often holds two or three jumbos that are waiting their turn.

Because some aircraft do not need the full facilities of the hangar interior, a nose-in facility has been built on to the eastern end of the hangar at mezzanine level, enabling lots of internal work to be done without taking up space inside. At the other end of the building, some distance away outside on the apron, is the engine run-up bay.

The whole site occupies 70 acres; the hangar floor area is 22,000 square metres and the mezzanine area 6,000 square metres. The support and administration buildings at the rear of the building, has an area of 16,000 square metres.

Total weight of steel	6,000 tonnes
Main spine beam	1,000 tonnes
Doors spine Beam	525 tonnes
Overall length of beams	233m

Depth of hangar	90m		
Highest point of hangar	33m		

It was designed to withstand winds of 100mph and the site has 600 car park spaces.

British Airways Fleet as of November 2000

Model	136	236	436
Length	232ft	232 ft	232ft
Wingspan	195ft	195ft	211ft
Max take-off weight	734,000lb	820,000lb	870,000lb
Engines	P&W JT9D-7	RB 211-524 D4	RB 211-524 H
Take-off thrust	45500lb/eng.	53100lb/eng.	60600lb/eng.
Max. usable fuel	39,309 gall.	44,850 gall.	47,718 gall.
BA seat configuration	376	373	383
Main checks			
Inter	5,750 hours	6,250 hours	6,250 hours
Major	24,000 hours/	24,000 hours/	24,000 hours/
	5 years	5 years	5 years
Fleet comprises	15	16	26
Total	57		

There were thirty-seven on order, plus twenty-six options. By the end of 2000 the maximum fleet was approximately 104, if all 436s were delivered and all 136s phased out.

The latest development at Cardiff International is the probable building of what is being termed as a centre of excellence in the aviation repair industry. DARA (Defence Aviation Repair Agency) after a long look at the ageing infrastructure at its headquarters at St Athan decided to move the greater part of its operations to a site across the runway to the British Airways repair hangar previously mentioned. The Welsh Development Agency unveiled a blue-print that would put a current 2,500 employees at the heart of this new initiative. Further jobs would be created by a cluster of other aerospace firms attracted by DARA and British Airways Maintenance. The proposed complex would be sited opposite BA, but consist of lower buildings than the BA facility to combat any environmental objections.

It was believed that the move from St Athan would not entail the station closing completely but that part of the workload that utilised the regular flying aspect of the airfield, such as the runway which has caused some trepidation for many years at the old RAF station, would be better served at Cardiff International airport. The vast workshops and other facilities at St Athan would still retain some engineers: after all the two airfields are but a couple of miles apart.

This was the situation in April 2001. It was abandoned in 2002 and new hangars are to be built at St Athan.

FIFTEEN

The Merthyr Tydfil Glider Field and Cubstrip

Grid Reference SO 007067, south of A465 Heads of the Valleys Road, near its junction with B4276 Bryn-y-Gwyddel

The glider field was on a plateau on the western side of Aberdare Mountain, now a thickly wooded defile in the forest. The site has great historical significance, the main interest probably being the Giants Grave, a cairn circle to the north of the landing ground.

This was to become the home of No.64 Glider School. There were five squadrons of the Air Training Corps between Treharris and Dowlais, and the school was to give air experience to those cadets with aircrew aspirations.

The ground was prepared by the members of No.415 (Merthyr Tydfil) and No.1813 (Merthyr Vale) Squadrons ATC. They levelled the surface and removed the stones – the larger ones were buried – eventually opening the field to flying in May 1944. The school suffered a setback, however, when the building that housed the gliders was burnt down. A blister hangar replaced it soon after and this survived for many years post-war, until the Forestry Commission moved in. No.1813 Squadron received an Avro 504 K biplane, but only for static use.

When units of the United States Army began to use the range on Mynedd-y-Glog, half a mile north of the glider field, near the Bavistock Hotel on the northern side of the A465, a requirement arose for the Air Observation Post's Piper Cub L4s. The exercises did not include field artillery, but tanks and mortars. The co-operation of the local authorities was sought and the use of the glider field was made available. Some say that not much use was made of it, and the cadets spoken to said that the Cubs were not based there but elsewhere. However, is attending only on weekends (as they did) the way to observe what went on during the weekdays on this fairly remote spot? It is difficult even today to find people who saw the landing and take-off activity at any of these cubstrips, because unless you had business there you were kept away, especially near to the ranges.

As with most of these units, come D-Day they were gone; only a few back-up battalions of Field Artillery were using the L4 after that in the UK.

No.1813 Squadron (Merthyr Vale) disbanded in July/August 1945 and their cadets transferred to No.415 (Merthyr Tydfil) Squadron, and this combination has survived up to now.

An interesting footnote to this period was sent by Mr C.H.C. Reed of Bridgend who writes:

This overhead, dated 13 April 1947, depicts the place where the glider and cub strip were situated which has unfortunately, since the war, been devastated first by open cast coal recovery and later forestation, so the strip can only be approximate in its marked position on the photograph. (Welsh Assembly Government Photographic Archive)

This Piper Cub, taking off in the mountains of northern Italy during the war, gives an impression of what it was like in the hills around the strip at Merthyr.

Opposite, top: The summit of Aberdare Mountain. Merthyr's western suburbs are to the right of picture and the landing area used by the Gliding school and the Piper Cubs was to the left, near the woods. The terrain has been bulldozed out of all shape of a runway. (Ivor Jones)

The 17-acre field at Gurnos Farm, Merthyr Tydfil, that played host to many Piper Cubs briefly in 1943. (Ivor Jones)

The 17-acre field at Gumos Farm on 13 April 1947. (Welsh Assembly Government Photographic Archive)

Vale of Glamorgan, Llandow, is visible at the top left of the photograph; St Athan in the lower middle; Rhoose at the bottom right. This was taken in 1947. (Welsh Assembly Government Archive)

During the war as a boy, I worked on the Gurnos Farm from 1941 to 1950.

One day in early 1944 my boss Mr Thomas told me to go to our biggest field, the 17 acre. This field was divided in two by a very old fence, that was rusty and broken. Mr Thomas told me to pull up the fence posts and roll up the wire and put in the corner of the field, together with any other rubbish there. This I did, and as it was Saturday I finished work at one o'clock.

By two o'clock that afternoon there were seven aircraft parked in the field, American Piper cub spotter planes. There were about twenty men with the planes, and they would come and go all day long for twelve days then, suddenly without any warning they were gone.

The field called 17 acres was opposite the Cefn Quarry, slightly uphill, the planes swept over the quarry to land. I asked Mr Thomas if he knew that they were coming and he said No.

It would appear that this was a temporary distribution point, used while the reconnaissance of the area was made for suitable landing sites in the locality. Gurnos Farm is also near the Heads of the Valleys Road, or its earlier equivalent, and is just north of Merthyr Tydfil, a few miles from the glider field, and the airstrip at Hirwain a few miles further along the A464 to the west.

SIXTEEN

Airfields at Llandrindod Wells

Grid Ref. SO 040605, south of the town and east of A483

The airstrip occupied a site on top of a hill that was also the location of the Llandrindod Golf Club and ancient cairns and standing stones. The club – founded in 1905 – had no knowledge of its use by the US Army, but in its meetings during the war a complaint against the Ministry of Defence was made, as an OCTU using the course was ripping up the road to the clubhouse. The Army at Brecon advised them that, as the course was to be requisitioned, the club would have its repairs done and be compensated post-war. This means that when the 196th Field Artillery Battalion moved into the golf course in late 1943, it was a Ministry of Defence site. I am advised that the hotel Metropole in the town was used as the battalion HQ and officers' quarters.

When the Piper Cub L4s of the battalion flew in it was to be a long programme of practice; more practice spotting in the new Air Observation Post, that the British had perfected in the desert and the Americans in North Africa, where the fall of shot delivered by the artillery is classified from up in the air in the L4, and corrections wirelessed down until a straddle is achieved. This unit was using either the Llangurig (Cambrian) Battle School to the west or the Mynedd Eppynt Artillery Range to the south.

It is not known when this unit left for the Continent, probably May or October 1944, leaving the golf club in peace.

Nobody has been able to remember anything of those days in this area; the museum, record office and newspaper have been left unusually bereft of knowledge. I have learnt more of an airstrip on a farmer's field, out in the wilds, than this one on a public amenity on the edge of a substantial town. The town did have a share in aviation though. In the late 1930s a firm attempt to establish an aerodrome on Ddole Field in the south of Llandrindod got as far as several air displays each summer, the last being in 1937. A gentleman named Tom Naughton was the main power behind these attempts. The field was used as a polo ground previously and later became a racecourse.

The mountaintop field used by the US Army's Cub L4s with the artillery units that stayed in Llandrindod. Facing west, the golf course is to the right in 2004. (Ivor Jones)

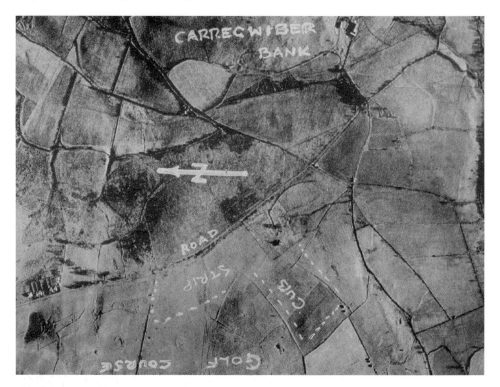

The airstrip on Little Hill, Llandrindod, in December 1946. Situated on what was then – and would be later on again – the golf club. The OCTU that occupied the club house and the fields, and later the American presence, left damaging marks on the club's roads and course. The strip is approximately 2 miles south-west of town. (Welsh Assembly Government Photographic Archive)

The last air display at Ddoll Airfield in 1937. (P.B. Abery)

Ddoll Airfield as it was: a racetrack, golf course, and showground, and it is still much the same as it was in the 1930s. To give an idea of the distance between Ddoll and the cubstrip, the strip is out of shot at the bottom right of this overhead of 4 December 1946. (Welsh Assembly Government Photographic Archive)

Ddoll Airfield in 2004 facing west. (Ivor Jones)

SEVENTEEN

RAF St Athan

Grid Reference ST 005685, 7 miles west of Barry, South Glamorgan

Like the vast majority of the Welsh military airfields, St Athan, or Sain Tathan in Welsh, is situated near to the sea on one side and near to the hills on the other. Some claim that it is the largest Royal Air Force base in the UK, covering an area of over 1,000 acres, and very large in terms of the personnel who have passed through the schools, camps and maintenance units. The number of aircraft that were stored, repaired, serviced, and modified here during the Second World War was enormous and the station continues doing this up to the present day.

The site, in a part of the Vale of Glamorgan that has a lot of tangible history bound up in it, was purchased in 1936. It lies between the east and west orchards, so named since the time of King Henry I, also an area where during the digging of the airfield's foundations, corroded daggers and other artefacts of Roman occupation were discovered.

Although the intention was to build a permanent RAF station in the usual grand style of the expansion period of the 1930s, in brick and stone, the political situation demanded that something be done urgently to accommodate the people and facilities needed, so the hutted camp was built as a temporary measure yet stayed to serve thousands of men up until the 1970s. The permanent buildings were built during the period 1939–41 and included a cinema to seat 1,200, a heated swimming pool, a huge gymnasium and an indoor drill hall.

A modern, well-equipped hospital was built outside the perimeter fence at the eastern end of the airfield. It served all the RAF stations in the south Wales area and was classified as a Regional Hospital. After the war it was also to serve the local civilian population, in the first years of the National Health Service. The medical staff doctors and nurses also formed the core of the Mountain Rescue Team that formed here.

The airfield is split into the west camp and the east camp with the grass landing area between them. Looking down on the airfield the two camps, each having their hangars nearest the field, formed in an arc around the perimeter track. In the west it is the C-Type hangars that are arrayed, in the east camp the Bellman hangars, all twenty of them until recently. They are now being demolished, one by one.

Lines of workshops lie behind the hangars in the same arc and behind all these are the stores and administration. Behind these were the accommodation blocks.

There are three dispersed sites on the station, the largest being Picketstone. It has two E-Type hangars and four B1-Types. This site lies to the north of the airfield proper and a good half-mile taxi-way connects it to the airfield perimeter track.

Another site is named Beggars Pound. It lies to the extreme south-east of the station and contains two E-type hangars. Bats Lays is another, also having two E-types, and is

All of the main
sites of the base
are in view in
1946, except for
Picketston which
can be seen later in
the chapter on the
St Athan taxi-track.
(Welsh Assembly
Government
Photographic
Archive)

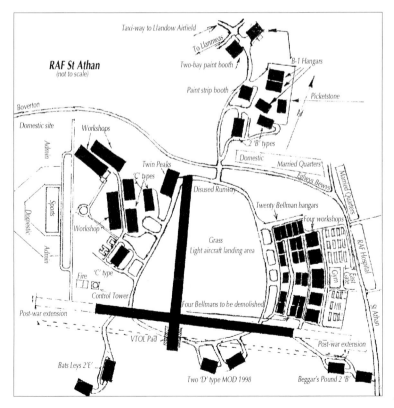

Map of the
St Athan sites and
runways. (Ivor
Jones)

The last of the huge hutted town at east camp that was built so hurriedly in 1938, mostly to house pupils of No.4 School of Technical Training. (Ivor Jones)

The hutted east camp early in its building. The hospital was not yet built.

situated at the south-west of the station. Drawing a line between the last two sites, to the south of the runway at the midway, is the site of the two D-types.

A contract was given to the Demolition & Construction Co. in the autumn of 1937 and the work was forced along at a fast pace because the Air Ministry had decided that the station would not be just a storage and maintenance facility, but would accommodate at least one training unit.

No.4 School of
Technical Training.
Budding flight engineers
receiving instruction on
a Lancaster cockpit.
(St Athan Archive)

No.4 School of Technical
Training, the hutted
camp at East Camp,
St Athan. (St Athan
Archive)

The Station Headquarters opened on 1 September 1939, just two days prior to the declaration of war by Britain against Germany. It was under the command of No.24 Group Training Command. The CO was Group Captain E.E. Rice.

The first unit to take up residence was No.4 School of Technical Training and this fine unit is still here to this day. This had come about because of the need to extract No.3 School of Technical Training from the airfield at Manston. This was to be a frontline fighter station and form part of the new No.4 School of Technical Training, which was to undertake the training of flight mechanics, flight riggers and drivers (petrol). Organised into five wings, it included the Station Headquarters, Accounting, Education, Equipment and Workshop sections, plus four Miles Magisters.

The new hutted camp prepared for the first intake under the command of Wing Commander J.J. Williamson AFC, bringing No.2 Training Wing and 1,000 trainees. The wing then split up into No.1, for flight rigger and flight mechanic training, plus drivers (petrol) and a small party of fifty-six naval air mechanics; No.3 Wing under the command of Wg Cdr E.R. Vaisey; No.4 Wing with a total, by the year's end, of seventy-one staff and twenty-nine civilian instructors. They also brought with them from Henlow the training aircraft, including Hawker Harts and Audax, Fairey 111Fs, Gordons, Blenheim 1s and Avro 504s.

There followed a rush of unit movements to evacuate training units from the south and east of England, leaving only operational squadrons at their bases. No.5 Salvage Centre, formed at St Athan on 18 September, then was hurried off to York on the 24th and renamed No.60 MU.

Avro Anson of No.1 School of Air Navigation at St Athan on 21 October 1939. K88l9/52 was one of a large fleet of sixty, plus thirty in reserve.

The DH Queen Bee arrived here as the equipment of the pilot-less Aircraft Unit, and later the aircraft of 'U' flight of No.1 Anti-Aircraft Co-operation Unit. These aircraft were operated from the ground by remote control and directed over the artillery ranges as a target. They came to St Athan for further electronic development.

On 21 October 1939, No.1 School of Navigation moved in from Manston in Kent away from the threat of air raids. They brought their establishment of sixty plus thirty Ansons. They set up their headquarters at West Cottage, North Barn, Eglwys Brewis, and the first intake of sixty air observer trainees arrived from North Coates. The flying programme of this unit was continuous, as the need of the RAF for navigators was great. Courses varied in length, the shortest being four days for an astro-navigation course, but there were diversions from the routine, such as the finding of enemy submarines in the course of their training flights. On 16 September 1939 Flying Officer Cohen in Anson L7967 sighted a submarine and three days later Pilot Officer McCarthy in Anson N4963 saw another. The following day two enemy submarines were attacked and sunk by Coastal Command aircraft in the same vicinity. The decision was made to arm the

The Miles Mentor was used with No.11 (Fighter) Group Pool at St Athan in the nervous days of late 1939. It was a two-seat trainer for the unit's Hurricane pilots. The unit was to be re-designated No.6 Operational Training Unit on 9 March 1940, based at St Athan for nine months, before moving to RAF Sutton Bridge.

school's aircraft with two 100lb bombs and to task them with maritime reconnaissance duties as well as their normal training commitments. Throughout December and January many more sightings were made, but then things quietened down until 16 August 1940 when Anson K6273 attacked a U-boat at 12:35 off Lundy Island without scoring any hits. Ansons K8827 and K8715 followed up the attack with no result.

After dark on 23 February 1940, with high winds, lashing rain and low cloud, Anson N5086 circled the airfield for a long time, trying to locate the flarepath. It made several attempts to land, but had to overshoot each time, and eventually flew away. Shortly afterwards an explosion was heard. The aircraft had flown into Rhossili Hill, a few miles inland and was wrecked with the loss of all on board. Then on 12 September 1940 Anson K6262 flew into the sea just before noon, again with the loss of all on board. The unit left for Canada to form No.31 ANS on 12 October 1940 at Port Albert Ontario, as part of the Empire Air Training Scheme.

The year 1939 was to see the introduction of many and varied units, and among the strangest was that of the pilot-less Aircraft Flight under No.70 Group, with the (Queen Bee) aircraft in the Anti-Aircraft Cooperation role. This unit had formed at RAF Henlow in 1937 but to continue the development of these radio-controlled artillery targets the engineering skills of St Athan were needed. This unit was to go into service at RAF Manorbier for the rest of the war, disbanding there on 15 March 1946.

The School of Motor Transport also arrived from Henlow as part of the School of Technical Training and a small supply and transport unit was formed here on 1 July 1939. As soon as war was declared, they transferred their vehicles to each of the five wings of the School of Technical Training and moved to France, picking up new vehicles at Wembley on the way. The School of Motor Transport moved to RAF Weeton near Blackpool in November 1939.

A Special Duties Flight was based here from November 1939 under No.24 Group Halton.

Also in November 1939 a Fighter Group Pool was installed in No.11 Group, equipped with Hurricanes and Mentors. They operated as the later Operational Training Units would, tasked with the urgent job of converting pilots to the Hurricane. Most of the pilots had been flying slow bi-planes, large and small, and now, with the aid of the early production Hurricanes with two bladed propellers of fixed pitch, they had to come up to speed. There were a few Miles Mentors, a couple of Battles, Tiger Moths and Harvards. No unit markings were carried but the Hurricanes had their flight colours painted on the spinners: 'A' flight was red, 'B' flight was blue and 'C' flight was yellow. In addition to training RAF pilots, they also trained 112 men from Finland. On 9 March 1940 No.11 Group Pool became No.6 Operational Training Unit and moved to Sutton Bridge, taking fifty-three Hurricanes and various other types with it after nine months at St Athan.

No.19 Maintenance Unit had been formed here on 7 February 1939 from the former Aircraft Storage Unit No.9 and became a civilian-manned MU, employing hundreds of people bussed in each day. It occupied eight hangars and many dispersal sites. The aircraft handled in those early days were Ansons, Battles, Blenheims, Defiants, Hampdens, Hurricanes, Lysanders and Tiger Moths, plus many others in small numbers, and by the end of 1939 there were 300 aircraft on charge, looked after by a staff of approximately 400.

No.32 MU formed here on 1 July 1939 as a Service Repair Depot with an Aircraft Repair Section, a Motor Transport Repair Section and General Engineering Section. This MU was manned by RAF personnel and continued under that name until disbandment on 1 November 1968, when it was then re-formed as an Aircraft Engineering Wing, with Nos 1, 2, 3, 4 and 10 Squadrons; a General Engineering Wing with Nos 5, 6, 7 and 8 Squadrons; Engineering Plans and Development with No.9 Squadron.

The Mountain Rescue team was also established at about this time, with doctors, nurses and motor transport dedicated to what was to become a brave and unselfish service.

By now the workload at St Athan was very heavy and the Aircraft Storage Units were overwhelmed. As the aircraft could not be safely hidden from enemy bombing, two Satellite Landing Grounds were acquired: one at St Brides (No.6 SLG) in April 1941 and one at Chepstow Racecourse (No.7 SLG) on 13 May 1941, where the aircraft could land and be hidden away in the woods about these places.

Another further attempt to foil the Luftwaffe was the building of a decoy airfield on the seashore between Aberthaw and Rhoose. It was a night-time only site with lights fixed on poles to simulate a Drem system flarepath.

Hurricane 1 of the 11 Group Pool overturned at St Athan. This unit was hastily converting old bi-plane pilots to the Hurricane fighter.

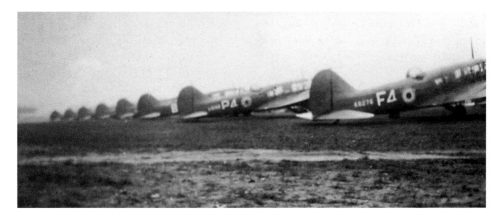

The Ansons of No.12 School of Wireless at St Athan. The unit was formed here on 17 July 1943 for ASV training, again with a large fleet of Ansons – 42 plus 21 in reserve.

The base had expanded so much by now that the post at St Athan was raised to Air Rank and the position of CO was given to Air Commodore the Hon. D. Boyle and No.4 School of Technical Training entered a new phase, a task that the advent of the four-engined bombers needed for a flight engineer on each aircraft, and the need to train them in their skills. By September the training of fitters and mechanics ceased. The initial recruitment of flight engineers was from the ranks of the airframe and engine fitters, and mechanics who had already received engineering training and would only need a short course. This was a temporary measure, and direct recruitment soon followed. By mid-1942, every allied flight engineer – apart from the Americans and Canadians who were trained elsewhere – all came through the gates of St Athan and for the rest of the war their training was the exclusive task of No.4 School of Technical Training.

No.12 Radio School was formed here on 1 September 1943 for ASV training with an establishment of forty-two plus twenty-one (reserve) Avro Ansons. It took over the preliminary training flights of No.7 OTU on 23 November 1943, the rest of No.7 OTU on 8 December 1943 and No.6 OTU of Coastal Command on the same date. This unit would eventually merge with No.14 Radio School to form the Empire Radio School on 7 March 1946. No.14 Radio School had formed here on 1 June 1944 and merged with No.12 RDS to form the ERS in March 1946, where wireless operators, radar operators, physical training instructors and navigators were taught.

The support to the MUs then, and still to this day, is provided by the workshops that abound at this base; I doubt whether there is another airbase like it. There is nothing that could not be reproduced in the machine shops or fitting, airframe and engine sheds, and turning, boring, milling and grinding of high precision parts goes on here now as it did sixty years ago.

An idea of the intense activity on the MUs in the early days is portrayed by the flying log of Flt Lt N.L. Tayler, DFC, one of the test pilots at St Athan. Between 1939 and the autumn of 1941 he was responsible for the testing of the following: fifteen Audaxes, twenty-four Hind trainers, one Hart trainer, four Avro Tutors, two Percival Gulls, two Mentors, 229 Magisters, forty-two Tiger Moths, five Gloster Gauntlets, six Harvards, thirty Queen Bees, ten Hectors, four Hudsons, one Hawker Demon, three Heyfords, seven Harrows, thirty-seven Lysanders, thirty-two Swordfish, one Dominie, twenty-three Skuas, eleven Vildebeests,

Officers' Mess at St Athan. (Ivor Jones)

B1 hangars at Picketston in 2002. During the war they were erected by the Ministry of Aircraft Production to cover the work of the Special Installations Unit at St Athans. (Ivor Jones)

one Northrop Nomad, one Hampden, eleven Ansons, twenty-eight Boston/Havocs, forty-five Bothas, ninety-five Defiants, twenty-two Beauforts, eleven Spitfires, eight Wellingtons, one Stirling, seventy-eight Battles, 136 Blenheims, ninety-eight Beaufighters and no fewer than 295 Hurricanes. On any one day he could do up to eight different types. The only one that he received instruction on was the Stirling.

The two MUs were hard-pressed and reached a peak in aircraft turnover in March 1941 when 187 aircraft were delivered to squadrons. New types, like the Mosquito and Mustang, were arriving, plus huge numbers of Spitfires, but the aspect of work done by No.32 MU that is least heard of was the ultra secret work of the Special Installations Section. This was concerned with the design, manufacture and fitting of radar aids to a wide variety of aircraft, from the Whitley to Lancaster and Catalina Halifax, amongst others. These aids were H2s, Rebecca, Gee, Loran, Oboe, Village Inn, Fish Pond and Monica. The work was carried out in great secrecy in three B1 hangars provided by the Ministry of Aircraft Production at a remote spot on the Picketstone site. All the personnel of the Special Installations Section received bicycles to get them to and from the site.

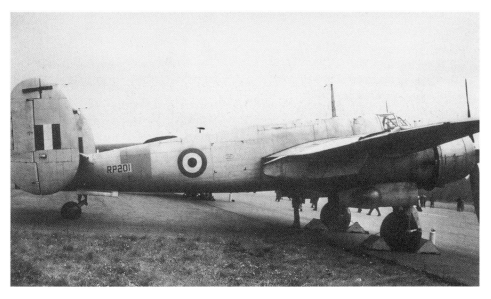

The Bristol Buckmaster Trainer was being delivered to St Athan for the installation of electronic devices to bring them up to service standard. Too late to serve in the war, many ended up at the MUs and stored until being 'reduced to produce' (the MOD expression for scrap).

From the beginning of the war there had been, a large contingent of our allies from France, Belgium and Poland, and especially Czechoslovakia, here before going to operational units. They had been placed here to attend instruction in the English language, attend No.4 School of Technical Training or to reform into ethnic groups. The Czechs were of a number to warrant a depot, which was established on 14 February 1942. Including pilots (fighter and bomber), observers, and wireless operators, they were gradually absorbed into the Czech squadrons of the RAF.

In early 1943 the RAF Regiment came on to the scene. Five sergeants and one corporal arrived from Halton to teach battle drill and unarmed combat to the permanent staff. Tuition was given in all machine guns, and bayonet drill.

When the war ended and the other stations were closing, RAF St Athan carried on. The main problem was the disposal of hundreds of unwanted aircraft; the land between the airfields of St Athan and Llandow was full of Lancasters, Halifaxes, Mosquitoes and so on. There were also new deliveries of types such as Brigands and Buckmasters. No.19 MU had the job of overhaul and storage of Vampires.

In 1946 a permanent Mountain Rescue Section was established here, with five permanent members of staff and all the rest of the manpower coming from volunteers. Their usual training area was the Brecon Beacons and the Black Mountains. Between 1946 and 1959 six aircraft crashed in the South Wales mountains and twenty-five in North Wales, and as a result of this the St Athan team was often required to assist the RAF Valley Mountain Rescue Team.

The School of Motor Transport was expanding here and by 1970 over 3,000 drivers were passing their tests each year.

In March 1947 No.68 ATC Gliding School arrived from Stormy Down but everything else was forgotten for a while as the British Empire and Commonwealth Games were held in Cardiff in the summer of 1958 and St Athan was given the job of providing the

The Bristol Brigand long-range attack aircraft. Awaiting collection at St Athan in December 1951, the Brigand would have the same fate as the Buckmaster.

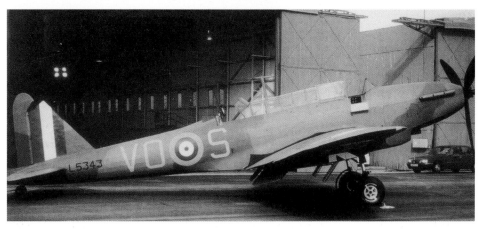

The St Athan aircraft collection, including Japanese and German war-planes, also had an excellent workshop with craftsmen experienced in the repair and refurbishment of these battered old aircraft. A Fairey Battle in around 1990 after several years of voluntary work, not long before the whole shebang was moved to Cosford or Hendon RAF Museum. (St Athan Archive)

accommodation to competitors and officials. The hutted site at Flemingstone, normally used by boy entrants, was taken over and the RAF hospital was made responsible for medical services.

St Athan had by now acquired many warplanes for themselves, not officially but on the strength that there were so many around being scrapped. Enemy warplanes were also diverted here at war's end so a very interesting museum was held in two, then three, of the Bellman hangars near the main runway. The hangars have now been demolished but up until 1990 one could visit this museum on one Sunday of each month. The museum's exhibits can now be seen at Cosford.

The School of Physical Education arrived post-war and stayed until moving to RAF Cosford in 1980, when the run-down in training began here to make way for pure engineering. The University of Wales Air Squadron that formed here in September 1963 is still here, equipped with Chipmunk T10s initially and then Bulldogs.

During the retirement of the Phantom from service, St Athan was engaged in stripping engines and so on before towing to the dump. Here are two F4Js – ZE355 the nearest – about to be towed away from the hangar doors. (St Athan Archive)

November 1968 saw major changes at St Athan. No.4 School of Technical Training became a lodger unit, and the identities of Nos 19 and 32 MUs disappeared, and they became simply squadrons on the base. What had been No.19 MU was now the Civilian Engineering Squadron.

As of 2000 there were approximately 1,200 RAF servicemen and women and approximately 2,460 civilians employed on the base and between them they have the respect of the MOD, passed down from those wartime years. They have never been out of the forefront of aero-engineering, but from 2001 they were required to tender for each new contract, in competition with the likes of British Aerospace and the Boeing Corporation. Under DARA (the Defence Aviation Repair Agency) they must compete in all the high technical advances in treatments such as non-destructive testing, paint finishes and stripping. Engine rebuilds are sometimes carried out here, sometimes supplied from outside.

The base has seen the deep servicing of all the RAF's frontline aircraft, the Canberra, Vulcan, Valiant and Victor, and when the Valiants were grounded with fatigue problems, they were all scrapped here. When the Government decided to finish with fixed wing aircraft in the Fleet Air Arm the Phantoms and Buccaneers were all disembarked; the Phantoms went to the RAF and the Buccaneers went into deep storage at St Athan, some making a re-appearance in the Gulf War.

St Athan is currently handling the deep servicing and repairs, plus modifications, to VC 10s, Harriers (both Navy and RAF), Jaguars, Hawks, Tornadoes GR I and F3. Tucanoes are also serviced here. The most interesting work here for the majority of the tradesmen is the vintage contracts to overhaul the likes of the Lancaster I City of Lincoln, which completed its repairs in the spring of 2000. The base also expects to receive helicopter work in the near future, both for the RAF and the Navy.

Resident flying units include the School of Technical Training, which has on charge Bulldog T1s 4 off, Gnats T1s, Jaguar GR1s, Jet Provost T3s and Jet Provost T5as. These are not aircraft in flying condition but instructional airframes. The University of Wales Air Squadron has until now been equipped with Bulldogs but they are about to be struck off charge and replaced by Grob Tutors. No.634 Volunteer Gliding Unit is flying Vikings, and can be seen swooping and soaring around most weekends.

The Support Command Defence School was based here for many years, but has now moved elsewhere. After many years of occupation the Motor Transport Drivers' School

August 1946 and St Athan is swamped with aircraft; all they need now are more Buckmasters. This is RP45 landing at the eastern end of the runway. The Bellman hangars have all either been demolished or are due to be. The two nearest, facing camera, Bellman hangars held the museum's aircraft from about 1950 until 1990. In view are Shackleton, Typhoon, Beaufighter, Oxford and Spitfire. (Mathew Brownlow)

The Battle of Britain flight received much tender loving care over the years at St Athan, but it seems that it is the Lancaster of that flight which spends the most time here. This is Lancaster B1 PA747 City of Lincoln landing on the east threshold at St Athan.

Canberra B2 outside the museum hangar. The aircraft was of No.10 Squadron and was to be preserved. The stripes around the aircraft were for the Suez Canal campaign.

A Vulcan landing at the station, where much work was done on this type.

The University of Wales Air Squadron with Scottish Aviation Bulldogs, in front of their Bellman hangar on East Camp. (Ivor Jones)

has moved elsewhere as part of a programme of clearance to concentrate on aviation engineering contracts.

There is a large apprentice facility in the civilian mode and, what with other aviation work in the near vicinity, such as the huge Boeing 747 maintenance hangar of British Airways at Cardiff International airport and their Avionics Plant at Llantrisant, plus General Electric's Engine Overhaul works at Caerphilly, aero-engineering is becoming a major employer in the area.

The Airfield & Buildings
There are six E-Type hangars and each has had its exterior walls lined all over their vast curved concrete tops with raised seam sheeting held in place by nylon straps that cross over from the concrete foundations where they are anchored to the other side, hooked

into the foundations again and, by the aid of a buckle with a ratchet, they are pulled down tight. This was all necessary as these sixty-year-old buildings were leaking and cracking with strange, ominous banging noises emanating from the old reinforcing bars inside the concrete walls and roof.

Two of the E-Types have also been refurbished inside. The white asbestos insulation that adorned the interior wall and roof has been blasted by water jets under high pressure until clean and then treated to a spray of a plastic/cement mix again under pressure. The floors have been resurfaced, new lighting, and the old heating system of pipework, fed from the boilerhouse outside the front of the hangar that is so typical of these Lamella types has been thrown out, to be replaced by ducting around the interior fed by a dehumidifier system that leaves the hangar dry and reasonably warm. It is intended to introduce this system to all the E-Types as money is made available.

The station has two D-Type hangars on the southern limits, on a separate site, and they have also been extensively refurbished. The curved roof has now got a new pitched one over the top of it. The walls, windows and doors have been modernised and together with a paint job they look like new.

The four C-Type hangars are feeling their age somewhat, and although they get their basic maintenance, they are unable to use the outer leaves of the doors as the gantries have all been condemned as unsafe due to corrosion. It so happens that the aircraft serviced in those hangars are not of sufficient wing span to be affected much, as the aircraft using these four hangars are Tornadoes. Building Nos 75 and 77 (the C-Types on the south and north) are deep servicing the GR1s. Building Nos 76 and 78 (the two C-Types in the middle of the group) handle the Fs.

With regard to the work at the two D-Types, the eastern one – Building No.D2 – handles the Jaguar and the D-Type to the west does the Harrier (building D1).

The two E-Type hangars (buildings Nos 54b and 55b) on the Beggars Pound site do the deep servicing and, more importantly, the MOD 2000. This MOD (modification) was a life extension programme to take the Hawk fleet through to its next ten-year

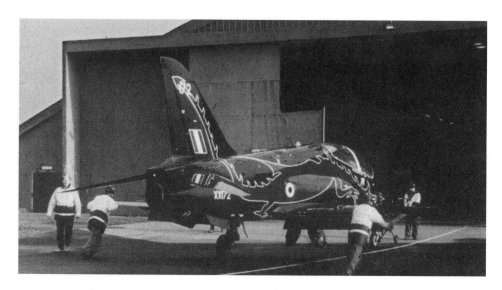

Another Hawk goes into the 'Beggars Pound' modernised E-type hangar. This aircraft had been used as a station hack by the delivery pilots at St Athan.

These buildings are the two D-type hangars on the south side of the airfield and main runway. The original curved roof of this type had been replaced with a pitched one on both hangars in 1999. (Ivor Jones)

Hipped C-type hangar on the west site at St Athan. (Ivor Jones)

A Jaguar inside a D-type hangar, undergoing maintenance. (Ivor Jones)

service and beyond. Depending on the fatigue life of the particular aircraft it will receive a new fuselage, as well as many other parts.

There were twenty Bellman hangars here at one time, reduced to sixteen some time ago and four more are to be demolished now. They have to be scrapped as it is only their proximity to one another and their mutual pipework, trunking and wiring keeping them up. So we shall soon be left with twelve. Two of these were in use in their later years. The enemy aircraft museum here sadly was removed to Cosford and Hendon. The remaining Bellmans house the aircraft of the University Air Squadron No.4 School of Technical Training's station Flight, the refuelling tankers and so on.

Latest in the hangar inventory is a newly erected large hangar for the servicing of VC10s, two at a time. Originally intended for Abingdon on its closure, it was built at St Athan as the VC10 contract had also been diverted here. Because of its appearance, and for the want of a better name, it has been named Twin Peaks. It is possible that the rumours are correct and it cost, with its jigs and fixtures, upwards of £5,500,000 to establish.

It is good to see many new buildings on the station. The RAF's latest hangar, to emulate the Blister, can be spotted. Known as RUBB, these are portable, of frame and rubber sheet covering, and can take an aircraft like a Hawk or Harrier. Many are in use in Bosnia.

Another type of hangar at this base is the B1, at the dispersed site at Picketstone, half a mile north-east of the airfield. There are four of them still doing super work – one is the vintage aircraft repair and paint shop, another is the apprentices' shop. Also at this site are two of the E-Types already mentioned, and this is where you find the 'crash & smash', as it is known on the base. Its real title is the Aircraft Recovery & Transportation Flight and the area contains the hulks of Canberras and Phantoms. Also at Picketstone is a new two-bay spray painting facility and a hangar where an aircraft's paint is removed under a type of sand-blasting but using Plastic Media. This site was the terminus of the longest taxi-way imaginable. It ran from the eastern end of the main runway of RAF Llandow, across two farms, through the dispersals of dozens of aircraft, heading for St Athan in a south-easterly direction for 3½ miles, delivering all types of aircraft. This went on in both directions for the last two years of the war.

This whole rather large dispersal area was well served with maintenance support. There were one Super Robin and ten Robin hangars distributed evenly about. The

The new hangar designed for the maintenance of the VC10. It has the unofficial name of Twin Peaks. (Ivor Jones)

The 'crash & smash' section on the Picketston site at St Athan. (Ivor Jones)

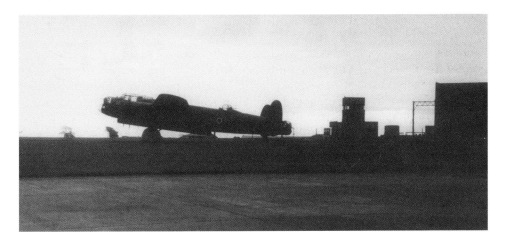

Battle of Britain Day, 1977. The Lancaster of BBMF outside the C-type hangar

Crash & Smash Flight was part of a larger unit, the Repair Support Squadron. Also in this were two important, highly skilled units. The Aircraft Repair Flight (ARF) comprised 103 riggers (airframe technicians) based around the country in teams of four and were the most highly trained and skilled in the RAF. The final unit was the Rear Support Flight who controlled the teams of ARF and also highly experienced technicians who surveyed the damage and made assessments.

I was not allowed to photograph the control tower close up for security reasons, but it is not of wartime vintage and appears to be of the 343/43 type and it is positioned on the north side of the western end of the runway.

The runways were developed gradually as needs arose. Originally a simple grass field surrounded by buildings, a Tarmac runway was laid on the south of the station in 1942. It ran east-north-east–west-north-west for a length of 1,200 yards. About a year later another was laid at right angles to the first, bisecting it at a point slightly more to the west of midway. This still left a large area of grass airfield for light aircraft to alight on

The old control tower photographed from the new tower at St Athan in August 1977. (David Lewis)

and take off from. Near to the end of the war the main runway was extended at both ends, requiring the moving of a road at its western end. These moves made the main runway 6,000ft long by 146ft wide.

The north–south runway is no longer used as such, just a taxi-way at its north end and its southern end is used as a VTOL pad for Harriers.

As well as the proliferation of hangars at this base, there are a lot of big workshops, both at the west camp and the east. Long lines of sheds, too numerous to discuss, prompted my guide to call St Athan 'an industrial estate with a runway'.

The station has a Unit Test Aircrew, comprising four pilots and two navigators. The CO is an RAF squadron leader but the rest civil service aircrew who have had extensive flying experience with the RAF, with an average of thirty years and 6,000 flying hours each. They are responsible for the ferrying of the aircraft to and from the user unit and the testing of each and every repaired, serviced or modified plane here. They do not consider themselves as test pilots in the popular image, as they never fly outside the aicraft's Flight Test Schedule (FTS).

A rather unusual episode occurred in the station's history when, in the summer of 1958, the hutted camp, ablutions, gymnasiums, pools and messes were used to accommodate hundreds of athletes involved in the Commonwealth Games which were being held in South Wales.

A few wartime pillboxes are about, together with air-raid shelters, but nowhere could we find the Picket Hamilton Forts that were reputed to exist.

Air Raids Upon St Athan 1940–42

Monday 15 July 1940 at 17:10: six bombs were dropped in two salvoes on the station. All the bombs fell on open ground and failed to explode.

Wednesday 18 July 1940 at 16:25: four bombs were dropped. Two exploded at the back of No.1 Workshop in the middle of the camp, near to the School of Navigation. Two huts were destroyed and there was damage to many others. Four RAF personnel were hurt. The third bomb fell on open ground causing no damage; the fourth also fell on open ground and failed to explode.

Monday 29–Tuesday 30 July 1940 at 01:15: a direct hit demolished No.109 married quarters. Luckily they were unoccupied.

Tuesday 6 August 1940 at 05:40: three HE bombs fell on the landing field adjoining the main site and damaged a hangar in the course of erection and also damaged two bombers on the field, a Blenheim and a Whitley.

Monday 19 August 1940 at 00:03: a direct hit on a hangar penetrated the roof and exploded inside. One aircraft was destroyed and two others damaged. Another bomb exploded on the apron.

Saturday 24 August 1940 at 21:00: four bombs dropped on the hutted campsite near the K-line huts and close to the School of Navigation. Part of the cookhouse was demolished, two huts were badly damaged, the water main fractured, and electric cables and heating pipes were damaged. Two bombs fell on open ground near the hospital causing no damage. Four bombs fell on the sports field near No.4 Wing with no damage. Then, shortly after, four more bombs were dropped resulting in the following: one direct hit on the x-ray room demolishing the building; one direct hit on the main entrance, demolishing it; one fell near the hospital and two wards were extensively damaged. Nine more H.E. bombs were dropped: two on the parade ground, one exploded behind the barrack block, three in front of the barrack block and three in the Demolition & Constructors Co.'s yard. The doors and windows of many buildings were damaged. A hit on the administration office demolished it. Six fell on the landing field causing large craters and yet another bomb fell on the hospital but was unexploded. Four further UXBs were found at other parts of the station.

A Red Arrows Folland Gnat in the spray shop, B1 hangar, on the Picketston site. (Ivor Jones)

Monday 12 May 1941 at 01:55: fourteen HE bombs were dropped and fell in the district of St Athan; five fell on the RAF station where damage was caused to Nos E3 and E4 hangars and aircraft in E4 were damaged. At the same time a delayed-action oil was also dropped and while four airmen were sandbagging it, it exploded killing all four.

2 July 1942 at 02:40: about twenty incendiary bombs were dropped on the station. No damage was caused.

The position at St Athan has changed since and large investments have secured the future of this base. The Defence Aviation Repair Agency (DARA) has built three new hangars joined together to make a large, handsome building, together with a support building and offices that will enable the company to maintain the RAF's aircraft in a more profitable manner than has been the case until now, when work was distributed between many sites at this old station. These old sites are to be taken on by the Welsh Development Agency in an attempt to bring more aviation work to the station.

The only ex-RAF hangar to be retained by DARA is the Abingdon Hangar, so called because of the gaining of the VC10 contract at this station when Abingdon was closed.

All the remainder of the old hangars are unwanted by DARA – B.1s, C-Types, Bellman, D-Types, E-Types – and are to be handed over to the WDA. The MOD, to help in this effort to take financial stress away from the management of DARA, has taken on the barracks and married quarters at West Camp to house the 1st Battalion Welsh Guards.

The new super-hangar will house DARA's head office and will provide over 45,000 square metres of hangar accommodation, along with 20,000 square metres of support workshops and office facilities. There will be a four-bay spray paint hangar, a two-bay paint and strip facility, engine test de-tuners, aircraft wash pad, fuel testing pad, compass swinging base and many other support facilities.

The Welsh Development Agency are to create what is to be named Aerospace Wales – St Athan, a centralised site that allows occupying organisations to share knowledge, create synergies and foster partnerships. In addition, potential customers will benefit from a pool of highly trained people who possess skills honed over many years of experience. The WDA propose to redevelop approximately 500 acres of the RAF site, and some additional adjoining land on a phased basis by replacing old outdated buildings with new purpose-built facilities. To ensure that DARA's strong skill base is not only maintained but enlarged, a world class aerospace training academy is due to be created by working with educational organisations such as Barry College International Centre for Aerospace Training.

The thing that would interest the aviation historian about this development is its proximity to a very important wartime site. The offices and the start of the hangars at the eastern end have been built in the yard of a centuries-old house, Eglwys Brwys, which was the headquarters of the Special Installations Section at St Athan. Based at the Picketston site in the B1 hangars provided by the Ministry of Aircraft Production, this place must have been one of the most important areas in the UK for a while, as almost every type of aircraft in RAF service had every conceivable electronic gadget that could be developed installed; H2S, Rebecca, Gee, Loran, Oboe, Village Inn, Fish Pond and Monica were fitted on this site. All that is in the past and the future is being constructed almost in its place.

The MOD/WDA agreement was completed on 30 November 2004 and the whole site transferred to the WDA on 1 April 2005 when it adopted all the old RAF sites. The title of this new agreement is the 'Red Dragon Project'.

Operation Red Dragon, as this huge development at DARA St Athan was called. This is the north facing wall of the new hangar block. Including offices and roads, it cost £80 million. (DARA)

The west facing fronts of hangars H1, H2 and H3 at DARA St Athan. (DARA)

The new hangar is huge and DARA expect it to accommodate seventy-five aircraft of the size of Tornados, Jaguars, Eurofighters, with liberal clearance between. It is interesting to compare another recent hangar built 2 miles away on Cardiff International Airport (the old RAF Rhoose) where British Airways built their own super-hangar to house three Boeing 747s or 777s. Opened in April 1993 it has been successful and rewarding to BA, and it too occupies a lot of space. Together with offices and support buildings it occupies

The interior of one of the new hangars of the Red Dragon project at St Athan. (DARA)

a 70-acre site. The hangar floor area is 22,000 square metres, the mezzanine floor is 6,000 square metres. The total weight of the steel is 6,000 tonnes and the hangar is 90m high. There are just two hangars with such a big future: at St Athan and Cardiff International.

Since August 2005 there has been a definite slump in optimism at DARA as the MOD has conceded to the RAF their argument that they cannot train their engineers how to look after the aircraft at the battle front if they do not work on them in peace time. As the aircraft at St Athan are maintained by civilians, and the more experienced fitters have retired from the squadron, then the job does not get done. The Harriers have already been taken back and now the Tornadoes are in danger of going.

Since then the fate of St Athan has been virtually decided and it seems that it will no longer be an air station for the RAF. In a statement published in the *Western Mail*, the MOD has decided to create an academy for the 'All In' training of not only the RAF but the Navy and Army too. This academy would need the accommodation and new hangars and other facilities that DARA has built and used, and the company's activities would cease at this place by 2007. The repair of aircraft will revert to RAF stations that are still operational.

Another site bidding for the academy is the RAF station at Cosford, but it is generally considered that St Athan has a very strong case and is the preferred option.

At a cost of £20 billion a consortium of Ratheon and Qinetec, plus the MOD, is to bring together the training of all three services, and this Metrix consortium, which also includes Land Securities, Laing O'Rourke, the Open University and EDS, has launched its bid for the Defence Training Contract. If successful, a giant building programme will begin and £14 billion will be invested over twenty-five years to house 5,000 military students, 1,500 civilian instructors and other support staff. As the closure of DARA will mean the loss of 500 skilled jobs, it is appropriate that this academy will go a long way to compensate for the loss of those jobs to this area.

EIGHTEEN

RAF Llandow

Grid Reference SS 960715

The Air Ministry, in its quest for more Aircraft Storage Units (ASU) in the late 1930s, decided to build one on this part of the Vale of Glamorgan. The land lies between Llantwit Major to the south and Cowbridge to the north. Both are towns of great age and historical interest.

Construction began in early 1939, on a field that had seen some flying by the occasional light aircraft, and in its formative years No.614 (Glamorgan) Squadron.of the Auxiliary Air Force used it occasionally at weekends for circuits and bumps, along with the airfield at Wenvoe, while Pengam Moors was being converted to RAF Cardiff.

Although the station was incomplete the first unit moved in on 1 April 1940. This was the service-manned No.38 Maintenance Unit (MU) which was to run a large Aircraft Storage Unit (ASU) using hangars that had yet to be built. First, one of the L-Type hangars and one runway were completed and aircraft arrived in numbers too large to accommodate. Eleven Super Robin hangars were rapidly erected on a temporary basis and more of the large L-Types were finished to handle the flow of Tiger Moths, Battles, Blenheims, Spitfires and Whitleys that had to be stored.

The station was allocated a decoy 'Q' site at Marcross about 2 miles south, near the sea, and the airmen of Llandow were to staff it when necessary. The station was under the control of No.41 Group and they allocated Llandow satellite landing grounds (SLG) at Rudbaxton in Pembrokeshire for the storage of surplus aircraft and to hide them from air attack. These were No.4 SLG from 1 May 1941 until Octobe 1941; No.5 SLG at Berrow (Worcester) from September 1942 to November 1944; No.7 SLG at Chepstow Racecourse from 27 October 1941 to May 1945.

They also used Haverfordwest, Weston-Super-Mare and Benson airfields to disperse the large numbers of aircraft they were receiving from the factories, maintenance units and Civilian Repair Companies.

By early 1943 seven L-Type storage hangars, three K-Type, one J-Type, two T2s, an A1 and twelve Blister hangars were built, and the aircraft types now included Albemarles, Bostons, Lancasters and Mustangs.

The first flying unit to arrive was No.53 Operational Training Unit from Heston. This had only recently been formed, with an establishment of twenty-seven plus nine Spitfires, ten plus four Masters and three plus one target tugs. It was only B flight that moved to Llandow on 26 June 1941, followed by the main party on 1 July 1941. A and C flights stayed on to form No.61 OTU at Heston. The commanding officer of the unit at Llandow was the famous Welshman, Wing Commander I.R.A. Jones, of First World War reputation. He went on to many commands in Wales.

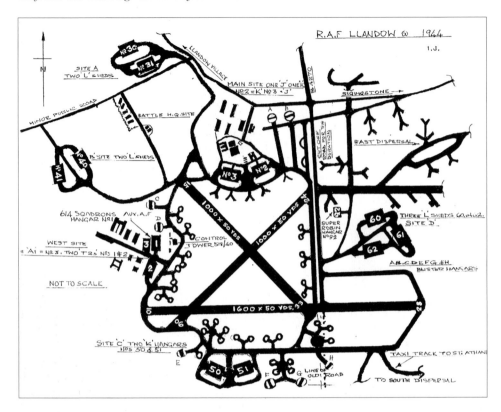

Map of the entire station, including runway lengths, and the connection to the famous taxi-track to St Athan at the bottom right of drawing. (Ivor Jones)

Spitfire 1 AR204, KU-Z, of No.53 OTU at Llandow in June 1942. There were no fewer than four codes allocated to No.53 OTU: MV, KU, OB and QG. (David Smith)

K-type hangar on C-site at Llandow. Aircraft storage unit, building No.50. (Ivor Jones)

This montage shows the many aircraft in the various dispersal areas in 1946, the peak time of aircraft destruction at RAF Llandow. Apart from the aircraft on this overhead, there are many more on the Llandow to St Athan track. (Welsh Assembly Government Photographic Archive)

Spitfire 1 OB-W undergoing re-painting of its roundels from A1 to C1, June 1942. No.53 Operational Training Unit at Llandow. (David Smith)

The OTU's task was the training of pilots who had completed their elementary and service flying training, the art of combat flying and dogfighting. During the two years that they operated from here, the locals became accustomed to pairs of Spitfires dog-fighting in the skies over the vale.

The unit grew to an establishment of fifty-one Spitfires with seventeen in reserve. These were mostly Mk 1s and 11s, and nearly all ex-Battle of Britain and war weary, but they would do for training. There were seventeen Masters, with five in reserve, and two Lysander Target tugs. On 7 April 1942 the OTU received its long-awaited satellite at Rhoose, where a lot of the unit's work was done from then on, as Llandow's runways were busy with the comings and goings of No.38 MU and the Aircraft Storage Unit. The aircraft of this unit ranged far and wide in their training, whether accidentally or on purpose, as crashes were reported a long way from Llandow. There was one such occasion on 7 June 1942 when a Spitfire of No.53 OTU was flying over Quinville on the Cherbourg Peninsula, France. The pupil pilot saw a motor vessel and attacked it, and was then chased by four Focke-Wulf 190s. Turning into them, he fired a two second burst which scattered them and enabled him to escape into the clouds. No.53 OTU's accident rate was high, partly because it was using war-weary Spitfires and partly because of the poor weather and visibility in the area of western coastline where they operated; but there were also lots of accidents on take-off and landing that had nothing to with the weather or the age of the aircraft. The unit lost over a hundred Spitfires while at Llandow.

Hundreds of pilots, especially Canadians and Australians, were trained here before the unit was posted to Kirton-in-Lindsay on 9 May 1943.

The replacement for No.53 OTU, on 1 July 1943, was the formation at Llandow of No.3 Overseas Aircraft Preparation Unit (OAPU). This was to prepare aircraft for onward travel and service in foreign climes, wherever they were needed. The planes were modified and ferried to the likes of Portreath in Cornwall to be flown off when the weather was fair, to destinations like Gibralter, Malta, Libya, Sicily, the Middle East and Italy. The types handled here were mostly Beaufighters, Wellingtons, Hudsons, Hampdens, Warwicks and Venturer Vs. It was re-designated No.3 Aircraft Preparation Unit from 5 July 1944.

They continued this work until August 1945, at which time the OAPU was transferred to Dunkeswell in Devon. The unit was renamed No.16 Ferry Unit on the same date.

Pilot, Sgt Donald Lowry-Boyd 404982 RAAF on No.12 course, No.53 OTU at Llandow, with Spitfire 1E behind him. (Phillip Davies)

No.53 OTU, May 1942. As well as the Spitfires parked on the left, another takes off over the Anson. (Phillip Davies)

It appears that a lot of aircraft overseas preparation work continued even after the departure of No.3 OAPU because the work seems to have carried on by No.38 MU. Up until the closure of Llandow, aircraft such as Lincolns, Lancasters, Shackletons and Mosquitoes were prepared by No.38 MU for the Malayan Emergency of the 1950s.

In March 1945, a large number of German POWs escaped from the Island Farm POW Camp at Bridgend and men from Llandow, St Athan and Stormy Down helped police during the days and nights to search the fields in the farms of the Vale of Glamorgan. They were all rounded up in a few days and three of these were captured in a pillbox on one of Llandow's dispersed sites.

Transport Command's Central Night Vision Training School was formed at Llandow on 21 April 1944.

Training crews for the civil flying experience were so vital if we were to challenge the USA at war's end. This was a joint exercise with BOAC. The unit moved to Ossington (Nottinghamshire) on 10 July 1945.

At the war's end, the airfield was swamped with suddenly unwanted aircraft, more than most stations. The fields surrounding Llandow became choked with Lancasters, Halifaxes, Wellingtons, Hamilcars, Spitfires, Beaufighters and Mosquitoes. By 1946 there were 856 aircraft on the books awaiting melting down.

Warden's office/
Guardroom building
No.18, main site at
Llandow. (Ivor Jones)

Control Tower/
Watch Office (Drng
No.518/40) on the
west site at Llandow
today. (Ivor Jones)

This Auster Autocrat G-AFWN, belonging to the Christie-Tylor furniture manufacturer, was leased
to Cambrian Air Services to make the very first post-war commercial flight from Pengam Moors to
Bristol (Filton). The photograph was taken outside the A1 hangar on the west site at Llandow. ('Ted'
Chamberlain)

Beaufighter
TT10 of No.4
CAACU (Civilian
Anti-Aircraft Co-
operation Unit) at
Llandow in 1951.
The man is Graham
Bowles, Tow Target
Operator, who was
employed by Short
Bros. (P. Davies)

Mosquito of No.4
CAACU had
undercarriage failure
at D-site, Llandow.
The pilot was
George Plinston
and the TTO was
Graham Bowles.

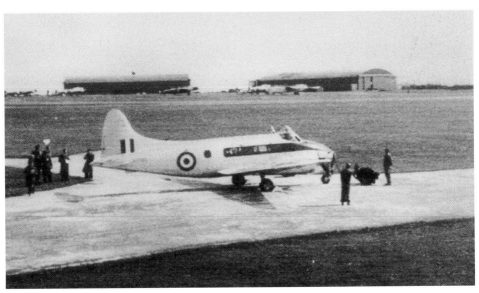

Prince Phillip's DH Dove in front of the Control Tower in 1950. The prince was on a visit to south
Wales. Note the Coastal Command Lancasters and the K-type hangars of C-site, Llandow. (P. Davies)

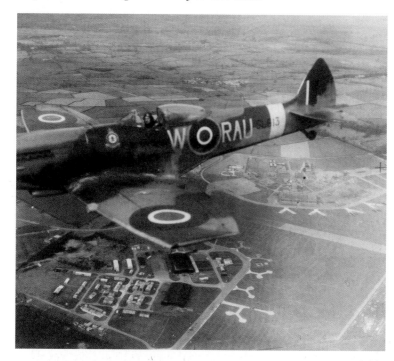

A No.614 Squadron Auxiliary Air Force (AAF) Spitfire Mk 22SL613 over Llandow Airfield in 1947. The pilot was Flt Lt George Martin. (P. Davies)

Another Spitfire Mk 22 of No.614 Squadron came to grief after touching down on runway 28. The reason for the undercarriage collapse has not been explained. (P. Davies)

On 1 August 1951 a new unit was formed at Llandow. This was the Civilian Anti-Aircraft Co-operation Unit (CAACU). These units were being formed to replace the service units that had towed targets for the Anti-Aircraft Gunnery Schools – in this case at Manorbier – and were ex-RAF flyers. The unit replaced service unit No 5 Squadron AACU and the new unit was numbered No.4 CAACU. It later joined No.3 CAACU at Exeter to form Nos 4–5 CAACU tasked with target towing or acting as targets for anti-aircraft gunners of the Army and Navy. Again there were accidents. They operated Spitfire 16s, Beaufighter TT 10s and Mosquitos. Mosquito TK 609 was involved in an accident when it swung to port on take off from Llandow. This was

RAF Llandow in June 1949, shows a No.614 Squadron fitter preparing Spitfire Mk 22 PK 667 for flight. ('Ted' Chamberlain)

Vampires of No.614 Squadron (County of Glamorgan) AAF taxiing to runway head No.10 *c.*1955. The T2 hangar on the left housed the aircraft of No.4 CAACU. The hangar used by No.614 Squadron is to the rear of this. Note the control tower on the right. ('Ted' Chamberlain)

corrected by throttle, but a slight swing to starboard started. After correction, this was followed by a pronounced swing to port, which took the Mosquito off the runway. As both throttles were closed and the brakes applied, the aircraft slid on the soft ground causing a crabbing movement, taking the Mosquito to the runway intersection where the starboard undercarriage collapsed and finally came to rest a hundred yards further on after ground looping. The pilot was unhurt.

Another later accident was that of the Vampire VT 820, flown by Flt Lt E. Whetter who was doing an air test on 16 June 1954. During the course of the test he did a victory roll over the airfield at 300–400ft and at high speed. The port wing bent upwards, followed by

No.614 Squadron's Vampires inside and outside their T2 hangar in 1952. They await refuelling. (P. Davies)

This is the site of the awful accident involving Flt Lt E. Whetter, who had performed an air test on Vampire VT820 on 16 June 1954. Losing lateral control, the aircraft first climbed and then dived at great speed. The aircraft crashed into the ground, making the crater pictured. Needless to say the poor man was killed. Note the aircraft parts across the airfield; it was totally shredded. (P. Davies)

a complete breakaway of two thirds of the wing. Parts struck the tail boom which caused it to break up and fall away. The aircraft then went into a high-speed roll to starboard, hit the ground and disintegrated, killing the pilot. This tragedy occurred at 14:42 and Mosquitoes in the nearby hangars were damaged by falling wreckage coming through the roof.

On 26 August 1947 No.614 Squadron Auxiliary Air Force re-formed at Llandow as a Fighter Squadron, ten years after its formation at Pengam Moors (Cardiff Airport) where it had been an Army Co-operation Squadron, then a Medium Bomber Squadron, a Heavy Bomber Squadron and then a Pathfinder Squadron operating from Italy over the Balkans. Re-formed as a fighter unit, it was equipped with Spitfire 16s and later with Mk 22s. In 1950 a Jet training programme was to see No.614 as a Vampire Squadron and that was their equipment until the disbandment of the auxiliary air force in 1957.

A flight of No.663 Squadron, in the Air Observation Post role in the Army Co-operation Unit, were based here from July 1949 till March 1957, flying Auster AOP 6s. With this, and No.614 Squadron's departure, the Royal Air Force Station Llandow was closed.

There was a tragedy here on 12 March 1950 when an Avro Tudor of Fairflight Ltd, registration no. G-AKBY crashed on its approach to Llandow's main runway when

D-Site aircraft storage unit and two of its L-type hangars, building Nos 61 and 62, in 2000. (Ivor Jones)

bringing back a crew of four and seventy-eight rugby supporters from Dublin after a Wales *v* Ireland international game. All of the crew and seventy-five of the passengers perished.

In March of 1945, while the war was still on, Glamorgan County Council received their long-awaited report on a scheme for an international airport for South Wales, produced by the county engineer John Powell, AM inst. CE, and what a splendid concept it was: a huge airfield utilising all the land of RAF Llandow and the land south to the outskirts of Llantwit Major and to the east and west of the present airfield. It all came to nothing of course.

The Airfield and Buildings at RAF Llandow

The runways were the usual three in number and were tarmac. The main runway lying east to west across the southern part of the airfield, marked 10/28, was 1,600 yards long. The north-east to south-west – 24/06 – was 1,000 yards long and the north-west to south-east runway, numbered 15/33, was also 1,000 yards long. A tarmac perimeter track connected them.

There were seven of the L-Type hangars, distributed to three dispersed sites. In a field in the north-west was site A with two, below that, to the west, was site B with two, and across the other side of the airfield was site D with three L-Types and one Super Robin. At the main unit site were one J- and one K-Type hangars. The west site carried two T2s and one A1 plus eight Blister hangars. South of the main runway lay site C with two K-Type and four Blister hangars.

The runways are still intact, but under a foot or two of soil with a few lengths exposed. The J-Type hangar was burned out and demolished many years ago. The T2s and A1, Robins and Blisters have gone, but all the L-Types and the three K-Types are extant.

The control tower (Drng No.518/40) is now the estate office. It is still in company with its wartime neighbours, such as the floodlight trailer shed, fire tender shelter and MT petrol installation of 1,000 gallons. The main site still has the impressive pre-war type warden's office and cycle park 2060/37, office block 2578/37, main workshops 2048/34, works services buildings with a well-preserved, high-level, brick-towered water tank, a typical main stores, canteen/NAAFI, decontamination block, and many others on the dispersed sites, such as standby set houses and pillboxes.

All of the hangars that remain are in use as retail outlets or as stores and there are a lot of small industrial firms, motor repair shops, tyre fitters and scrap vehicle yards. A go-kart track occupies part of the southern airfield.

The main workshops on the main site at Llandow in 2000, with the water tower to the rear. (Ivor Jones)

There are two memorials at Llandow, one at the roadside of B4270, the road that runs north–south through the airfield and once comprised the eastern perimeter-track, the other just a couple of hundred yards to the east of the main runway, where the Avro Tudor crashed at the village of Sigingstone. The first mentioned memorial is to the young men who died flying with No.53 OTU and with No.4 CAACU.

Air Raids on Llandow

On Monday 15 July 1940 at 17:20, four bombs were dropped and exploded on the station. Apart from damage to roofs and breaking the windows of a few huts, there was no damage and no injuries.

On 28 November 1941 at 19:50, two parachute mines were dropped and exploded in a boggy area at the airfield. Damage was caused to a hangar and the roofs and windows of several buildings. Eight wooden huts were completely demolished and several others extensively damaged. Of the casualties, one was serious and sixteen were slightly injured. The electricity supply to the airfield and the surrounding area was affected for a few hours.

At the eastern end of Llandow's main runway, its peri-track makes a junction with a track pointing south. This track is now barred by a farm gate, but from the middle of the Second World War it was a taxi-way that wound its way through large aircraft dispersals, across two farms and two roads, until it reached the outer dispersal of RAF St Athan, some 2–3 miles away at Picketstone. This allowed any aircraft to move from St Athan to Llandow, and of course vice versa. The fields between these three busy MUs, No.38 at Llandow and Nos 19 and 32 at St Athan, were packed with aircraft of all types.

Mr Ted Chamberlain, who was serving at Llandow, firstly with No.38 MU and later with No.614 Squadron AAF, assures me that it was not only the smaller types of aircraft that used this long track. Lancasters and Halifaxes also used it because the runway at St Athan was not long enough to suit most pilots, and this was not altered until the war's end. For the most part, if the larger aircraft were to be delivered to St Athan, it would be preferable to land on the main runway at Llandow and be towed to the place of delivery.

Mr George Checketts, ex-Wireless Operator-Airgunner and a much travelled airman, found a job with No.38 MU at Llandow after leaving the RAF in the 1949–50 period when the airfield was still busy and still had seven years left to run. He gave me a rough idea as to what use the hangars and other facilities here were put in those years before closure. He said that the main site hangar, No.2, was working on Meteors and Vampires

Building No.17
on the main site at
Llandow: the station
offices. (Ivor Jones)

and No.3 hangar was all Lancaster work. The L-Types were storing cocooned Lancasters up on Site A. The engines were emptied and inhibited; all loose radio or radar systems were extracted and were kept until needed or scrapped.

Overseas preparation work was carried out in the two K-Type hangars on site C, south of the main runway. Work in the nature of modification to Shackletons, and Lincolns, on aircraft straight from the manufacturers was carried out here.

Hangar No.1, a T2, was to end its life as the hangar of No.614 Squadron. No.2 was to house the aircraft of No.4 CAACU. The A1 hangar was busy servicing light aircraft. This is a well-preserved example of a pre-war design airfield, as there is still so much left to see even though it is occupied by farmers and small industries.

No.53 OTU formed on 18 February 1941 at Heston and moved on 1 July 1941 to Llandow. (Only B flight moved; A and C flights remained at Heston to form No.61 OTU.) The unit used the Satellite Landing Ground at Rhoose between 7 April 1942–May 1943 and Hibaldstow May 1943–May 1945, before moving to Kirton-in-Lindsey on 9 May 1943 and disbanding on 15 May 1945. No.53 OTU was allocated the code Letters MV and QG.

Aircraft of No.52 OTU at Llandow
Spitfire 1

K 9799, 9801, 9803, 9817, 9823, 9850, 9852, 9862, 9865, 9871, 9873, 9887, 9891, 9899, 9900, 9904, 9918, 9924, 9930, 9933, 9940, 9942, 9951, 9976, 9997.

L 1009, 1014, 1021, 1024, 1027, 1038, 1041, 1054, 1061, 1065, 1071, 1073, 1080, 1096.

N 3037, 3045, 3046, 3058, 3094, 3119, 3124, 3163, 3174, 3178, 3199, 3221, 3228, 3230, 3246, 3247, 3279, 3283.

P 9318, 9322, 9326, 9332, 9335, 9368, 9371, 9375, 9376, 9380, 9393, 9387, 9425, 9432, 9444, 9445, 9448, 9459, 9462, 9468, 9490, 9491, 9500, 9509, 9513, 9595, 9549, 9556, 9563.

R 6602, 6606, 6621, 6639, 6641, 6684, 6706, 6712, 6716, 6762, 6763, 6771, 6777, 6803, 6815, 6817, 6835, 6837, 6895, 6916, 6924, 6963, 6965, 6969, 6972, 6976, 6979, 6986, 6992, 6996, 7017, 7022, 7057, 7063, 7067, 7072, 7124, 7159, 7162, 7202, 7251, 7252.

X 4010, 4015, 4023, 4024, 4051, 4067, 4104, 4105, 4163, 4174, 4175, 4232, 4246, 4255, 4258, 4263, 4266, 4337, 4338, 4341, 4343, 4344, 4346, 4353, 4381, 4382, 4389, 4390, 4415, 4416, 4427, 4472, 4474, 4477, 4478, 4480, 4481, 4489, 4546, 4551, 4558, 4587, 4588, 4598, 4601, 4602, 4606, 4607, 4612, 4614, 4616, 4618, 4641, 4644, 4648, 4654, 4656, 4659, 4661, 4674,- 4677, 4679, 4683, 4719,- 4722, 4765, 4767, - 4769, 4771,

    - 4775, 4779, 4781, 4783, 4785, 4788, 4818, -- 4820, 4823, 4827, 4830, 4833, 4834, 4847, 4849, 4854, 4857, 4897, 4900, 4901, 4909, 4912, 4913, 4925, 4934, 4935, 4938, 4940, 4988, 4990, 4993, 4996.

AR 213, 215, 223, 225, 228, 229, 237, 247, 249, 253, 255.

Spitfire IIa
P   7288, 7293, 7294, 7297, 7310, 7315, 7316, 7320, 7357, 7367, 7372, 7377, 7378, 7389, 7434, 7442, 7494, 7503, 7504, 7553, 7554, 7557, 7563, 7595, 7602, 7604, 7607, 7623, 7660, 7663, 7667, 7674, 7681, 7687, 7742, 7747, 7754, 7772, 7781, 7782, 7820, 7822, 7826, 7827, 7829, 7840, 7885, 7895, 7903, 7910, 7915, 7920, 7921, 7926, 7927, 7929, 7983, 7985, 7988, 7989, 7996, 7998, 8012, 8014, 8020, 8025, 8038, 8071, 8072, 8075, 8081, 8087, 8096, 8133, 8134, 8168, 8186, 8189, 8191, 8192, 8193, 8196, 8200, 8201, 8235, 8238, 8239, 8249, 8271, 8274, 8278, 8317, 8336, 8338, 8341, 8349, 8366, 8367, 8371, 8372, 8373, 8375, 8380, 8396, 8423, 8431, 8432, 8475, 8508, 8514, 8527, 8528, 8533, 8568, 8570, 8575, 8579, 8592, 8598, 8641, 8652, 8673, 8692, 8704.

Spitfire Va and Vb
R   6720, 6801.
W   3228, 3250, 3305, 3313, 3375, 3380, 3640, 3718, 3759, 3837, 'X' 4671.
AA 738, 842, 915, 916, 931, 972.
AB 212, 509, 524, 782, 790, 904, 910, 974, 986.
AD 295, 317, 386, 576.
AR 614.
BL 259, 370, 464, 472, 473, 541, 669, 755, 788, 862, 966, 979.
BM 155, 198, 205, 233, 304, 348, 351, 354, 358, 369, 459, 565, 480, 490, 530, 537, 567, 572, 641, 645.
BR 160.

Spitfire IX
BS 395.

Fairy Battle
L   5713, 5749, 5781.

Miles Master I/III/II
N   7416, 7424, 7451, 7486, 7493, 7510, 7515, 7536, 7608, 7620, 7631, 7635, 7676, 7680, 7681, 7692, 7699, 7719, 7773, 7778, 7841, 7842, 7890, 7943, 7953, 7964, 7969, 8045.
T   8330, 8339, 8611, 8628, 8750, 8766, 8769, 8770, 8771, 8776.
W   8566, 8577, 8587–8591, 8597, 8629, 8636, 8638, 8639, 8641, 8649, 8658, 8695, 8696– 8699, 8700, 8861, 8889, 8952, 9072, 9074.
AZ 282, 529, 591, 592, 602, 778, 849.

Westland Lysander II/III
P   1681, 1698.
R   1990.
T   1566, 1610, 1681, 1766.
V   9752.

NINETEEN

Llandow to St Athan Taxi-way

It is approximately 2 miles as the crow flies from the eastern end of RAF Llandow's main runway to the most northern part of the Picketston Site of RAF St Athan. Between these two places a dispersal area developed there between the airfields, with winding tracks through the fields of farms such as Pleasant View, Park Farm, Brook Farm, Ty-Draw, and Great House Farm. In most cases the starburst, pan handle and loops covering these meadows are still there under a foot of soil and turf.

These dispersed aircraft, overflowed from the MUs at the two stations, had begun in around late 1941, as unwanted types of aircraft were swamping lots of other airfields. However, there were not only unwanted aircraft, indeed there is evidence of new work being carried out on these dispersals.

There were twenty Robin and Super Robin Hangars distributed about the fields, and No.19 MU's personnel and No.32 MU's servicemen worked from them.

These tracks carried two-way traffic between the two stations, and they fed the many storage areas. In the early years it was the single-engined, or at most twin-engined, types that were accommodated, but as the four-engined aircraft came into service, so the area slowly filled with these, until at war's end the fields around both stations were crammed with the likes of Lancasters and Halifaxes.

It was in 1946–1949 that an orgy of aircraft destruction took place here, in these now quiet meadows, and it seems odd that such a thing could have occurred. When looking back many people believe that sales abroad and the need for conservation of these historic aircraft would have given many of them a good home. The smaller aircraft – Mosquitoes, Spitfires, Mustangs, Hurricanes – would fetch a fine price now. The large looped dispersal near the village of Sigingstone is the place where the cutting up took place (see top photograph overleaf).

The two-way traffic was not apparently even. In the era of the large four-engine types there was some reluctance by the ferry pilots to land at the short, crowded St Athan runway, preferring the superior main runway of Llandow, and to have the aircraft towed to St Athan via the taxi-way.

In fact, the main Llandow runway had always been the night landing runway for aircraft making for St Athan as the latter had no flarepath or runway lighting at all. Mr Ted Chamberlain served with the Signals Section of No.38 MU at Llandow between 1951 and 1954. His job was as radio telephone direction finder in a building 200 yards away on the runway centre line west. When he left the RAF he joined No.614 Squadron Auxiliary Air Force at Llandow doing much the same work and control tower duty. Ted is a fountain of knowledge and has a fine memory. When I referred to the matter of runways, he told me of an occasion when an Avro York was to be ferried in to St Athan and the pilot decided after a good look around, that he would rather

This composite of overlapping Photographic Reconnaissance Unit (PRU) photographs shows the extent of the dispersals here. The two stations had several fields to use, filled with unwanted aircraft, but this one was shared. Aircraft were taxied or towed between the two stations. The PRU photographs were taken in August 1945, not by any means their busiest time. St Athan's Picketston site is at the bottom left. Llandow's main runway is at the top right. (Welsh Assembly Government Photographic Archive)

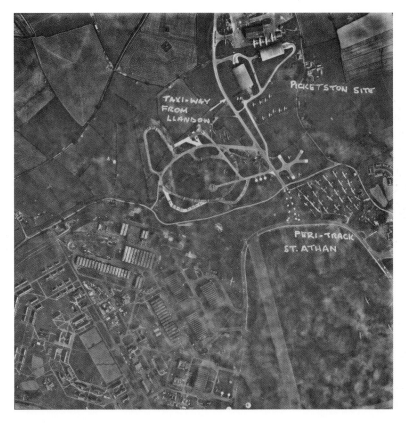

This overhead shows the beginning of the Picketston site as the taxi-way winds up from the St Athan perimeter track. (Welsh Assembly Government Photographic Archive)

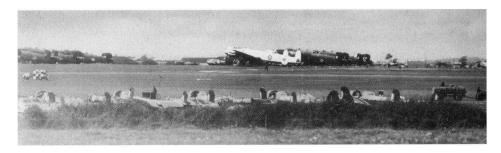

Lancasters and Halifaxes in rows in the field just north of the hangars on Picketston site on 14 August 1946. Note the rows of fuselages and empennages in the foreground. (Mathew Brownlow)

Albemarle on the dump on 9 April 1946. (The Hodgekiss Collection)

Beaufighter QM-C ex-No.254 Squadron. Awaiting destruction on 9 November 1947. (The Hodgekiss Collection)

land at Llandow, which he did. Serving with No.38 MU at Llandow in that period was a Master pilot who had a record of having flown a hundred types of aircraft. He scornfully listened to this chap's moans, took off from Llandow and went straight over and landed at St Athan successfully, to have a job done on it. That is where it stayed, as no one wanted to fly it out. It stayed for the rest of its days at the School of Technical Training as an instructional airframe.

Mr David Parker of Green Farm was also able to remember the period when his fields and others were occupied by aircraft. He said that some of the farms refused to

Above: Mosquito P-YH ex-No.215 Squadron on 9 November 1947. (The Hodgekiss Collection)

Left: Boston/Havoc on the scrapping field at Sigingstone, near Llandow, on 20 June 1947. (The Hodgekiss Collection)

have concrete taxi-ways laid over their ground but did settle for the square mesh/steel track option. When they lifted this track it was under many inches of earth and tangled grass and was hard work. The longest piece of steel tracking was south of the large loop dispersal near Sigingstone.

Mr Parker confirms what Mr Chamberlain said regarding flying into Llandow, even for aircraft bound for St Athan, and further states that although there was a lot of work in engineering, avionics, and radio, requiring landings at St Athan, the flying taking place there was only a quarter of that at Llandow. His most vivid memories were of the take-offs and landings of Shackletons and Canberras and, later, the Vampires of No.614 Squadron. He showed me where the jet engines were run up with wheel brakes on for take-off – the white burn marks are still there, at the east end of the main runway – then the detachment of Lincolns from Scampton that ran into the boundary bank near the railway line at the western end of the runway at St Athan in 1951.

The top photograph on page 123 shows Lancasters and Halifaxes on the field north-west of the B1 hangars at the Picketston Dispersed Site. Hangar B4 is low to the left; hangars B1, 2 and 3 are to the right of that and across the field to the far right is Splott Cottage, now demolished.

These meadows between RAF St Athan and the now defunct RAF Llandow have returned to agriculture, but there are tell-tale signs of their use in wartime, and for a few post-war years, of the millions of pounds' worth of aircraft destroyed here.

TWENTY

St Mary Hill Camp Cubstrip

Grid Reference SS 974795, Vale of Glamorgan

This was erected on Mynedd Ruthin Common in a rush to host the many American Army units that were arriving in South Wales to act as follow-up forces after D-Day, the first of whom arrived at Christmas 1943. The lower ranks were in tents with a layer of gravel from the nearby quarry as a floor on top of the wet, cold moorland soil. The officers were also in tents but on concrete slabs covering the area of floor in the tent. More permanent buildings were built for messing, stores, and administration blocks.

Several units made this their home and exercise areas to the south enabled a baseball diamond and other facilities to be used for recreation, and maintain fitness. The local children watched it all and made friends with the generous newcomers.

The troops, in their leisure time, would spend their money in Pencoed and Bridgend, where enough people of the opposite sex were available to provide company at dances organised by the Americans. Many relationships were formed, even resulting in a few GI brides. The camp was protected and guarded by troops of the British Army, the perimeter was fenced and sometimes crossed over the paths leading from some farms and houses, preventing access to the schools and the buses that were necessary to the local people, so they were escorted by an American soldier to the fence at the camp's entrance to be handed over to a British soldier who was to see them off the site.

Late on the scene came two units, 319th and 320th Field Artillery Battalions of the US Army on 25 May 1944, staying only until 3 June, before joining with others in a vast convoy that was to stretch for miles down the country road, witnessed by the locals, who had enjoyed the company of these lads for half a year.

After the Americans had vacated the camp it was decided to bring all the lower ranks of German POWs from the nearby Island Farm Camp to St Mary's, so that Island Camp would be strictly for officers only. At the end of the hostilities, a slow return to Germany for those who wished to began, but it took many years to complete (about 1948 is the nearest that one can assume).

When these wartime needs had been met, and the place lay empty, the local authority's troubles began with the emergence of squatters, and it was due to their presence and the troubles caused that the camp was demolished.

My interest in this camp is confined to any potential airstrip used by the Field Artillery Battalions that stayed – albeit briefly – and any liaison or communication flights made from here. It was hard to find anybody to confirm that aircraft were here at all, as there are few people in this thinly populated area of the age to have witnessed the rare comings and goings of light aircraft. Possible sites were studied and none had been

St Mary Hill camp can be seen at the foot of this RAF overhead on 25 September 1945, only fifteen months after the US Army had vacated the camp. The airstrip is north of the camp, in the 30-acre field. Note the concrete bases of huts at the bottom of the airfield near the gate. The M4 motorway now crosses the 30-acre field in a west–east line. (Welsh Assembly Government Photographic Archive)

The high ground to the right of the road was the approximate camp centre. At the foot of picture, on the right, is the lead in to the camp. (Ivor Jones)

The Piper Cub L4, Air Observation Post, was the aircraft that followed wherever the Field Artillery Battalion went, two to each battalion.

St Mary Hill Golf Course in 2006. At one time it was a meadow, then, very briefly, an airstrip. It once belonged to Breigam Farm but was absorbed into the lands of Trallwm for the purpose of establishing a golf course. This photograph shows the top of the gradient that leads up from the hotel and clubhouse. A lot of soil was moved around in fixing the holes and hazards, and the trees and shrubs have been planted over the last ten years. The M4 is 200m behind the photographer.

confirmed until, in answer to appeals made in letters sent to selected farmers, I received the help required.

My letter to one former farmer struck a chord. After his acquisition of Trallwm Farm, he made a golf course of the land and a fine hotel on the site of the now demolished farmhouse. This later attracted him to another purchase of land to the east of the hotel to build a further twelve-hole course on, and this was the field that was used by the aircraft of the US Army at the camp of St Mary Hill.

Known to the local farmers as the 30-acre field – the largest area of flat grassland for miles around – when the buyer of this field made his survey he thought of it as a fine potential airfield for light aircraft, and on receiving my appeal by letter he contacted the gentleman who was a youth at the time but remembers the occasional landing on what was then a fine flat field.

Mr Gwyn Jones is the owner of these golf courses, the hotel and restaurant. He is also an aviator and had vague ideas in the past about making an airfield of his land but thought better of it. The youth who became the only witness was Mr Tom Harry who was still able to talk to me of those interesting times sixty years ago.

TWENTY-ONE

Airstrip at St Donats Castle and Marcross

Grid Reference SS 936680, Vale of Glamorgan

As happened at other castles and manorial houses in Wales in the build up to the landings in Normandy, the US Army requisitioned the estate of St Donats Castle and that included a fine position on the beach, as well as a large stretch of land to the west and east of the castle.

The earliest parts of the castle were built in the twelfth century by the de Hawey family, who lived here until, through marriage, it passed to the Stradlings who then lived here for 440 years. After passing through other hands, it was bought up by William Randolph Hearst – the American publishing millionaire – and it was in his company's ownership when war broke out.

The British War Office rushed to take over the castle in October 1939 to house the 2nd/5th Battalion Welch Regiment, then an officers' training unit, took over the site in 1940. This was followed by an induction course for the first of many conscripts for the ATS (Auxiliary Territorial Service) which occupied St Donats, but it was the presence of the US Army in its various forms here that brought attention from the local population. They also brought about the small landing ground for the use by the Air Observation Post aircraft, the Piper Cub L4s of the artillery battalions that were based here and other liaison flights into and out of the field known as King George's field for some reason, even if only for a short period of time.

The first of these units was elements of the 28th Infantry Division and upon that unit's departure, artillery batteries of the 90th Division rotated through. It would appear that training on the Sennybridge ranges was the factor.

The 2nd Division had replaced the 28th in the D-Day landing follow-up force and had been brought from Armagh, Northern Ireland, first to Tenby and then to St Donats on 15 May 1944, staying only until their departure to Normandy on 7 June 1944.

One of this division's units was the 12th Field Artillery Battalion and, of course, they brought their Cub L4s. The fact that this was now the Division Command Post meant that there was, in addition to the gun-laying exercises to fly, Divisional Air Liaison and visitor flights to accommodate on this very suitable airfield. Running parallel to the road to Llantwit Major, it has the sea to the south and to its west are the trees that camouflaged the huts and tents of what is remembered locally as 'The American Camp'.

After the D-Day landings, some of the injured US troops who had already received hospital treatment were sent to St Donats to convalesce and delighted in the tales of Randolph Hearst's occupancy of this very beautiful place with Marion Davies. The

St Donats. This US Air Force PRU overhead shows both of the landing grounds in one photograph. The Q-site of Marcross Airfield is at the top and the cubstrip is at the bottom near the sea. The castle is shrouded in trees, but the swimming pool is the rectangle just off the beach. (Welsh Assembly Government Photographic Archive)

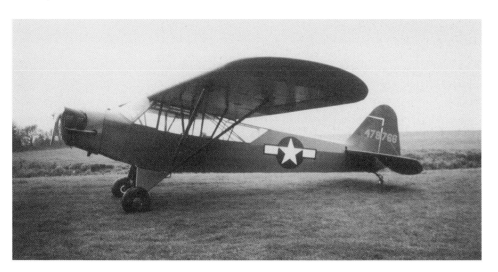

This Piper Cub belongs to Mr Kenneth Wakefield, ex-captain of Cambrian Airways, and author of many aviation and military books. This aircraft of his actually saw service, and action in Normandy and elsewhere on the continent. This is the type of aircraft that would have been at St Donats Castle.

accommodation for the troops was mostly the typical square-based bell tents that were dispersed along the roads, hedges and tree-lines of the castle grounds, with more substantial huts for messing, kitchens, drying rooms, shower blocks and ablutions. To give some scale to the arrival and accommodation of a unit such as the 12th FA Battalion, here are the numbers:

HQ Battery	23 officers	99 men
A Battery	23 officers	99 men
B Battery	23 officers	99 men
C Battery	23 officers	99 men
Service Company	27 officers	67 men
Medical Detachment	3 officers	12 men
Total	122 officers	475 men

The unit's movements were rapid and frequent, causing the tent population to grow and shrink with these movements, and yet some men stayed for some time here – long enough to make substantial relationships with the people of Llantwit Major and its pubs.

The locals seemed to have a warm relationship with the GIs, as evoked by this poem, written by a local lady who was a bus conductor on the very route that passed the camp, and on to Llantwit.

A Tribute to the Doughboys, by Grace Greenslade Burnet.

The story of a Castle,
A war time tale,
Memories of World War II
And of the beautiful Vale.

St Donats Castle
Once owned by Randolph Hearst
A friendly invasion of American troops
So crowded the walls might burst.

Fascination for me,
Then quite a young lass,
A 'Clippy' on a bus,
Which was run on gas.

The sight of the 'Doughboys'
Trooping out of that Castle
Bustling, noisy, but–
Causing no hassle.
On the evening bus service
They would clamour for a ride,-
To the nearest, little ancient town
Uniforms immaculate,
And worn with pride.

This is the sports field at St Donats, now Atlantic College, looking east with the sea to the right. For brief periods it was in use by light liaison aircraft of several units. (Ivor Jones)

A bus filled to capacity
Of cheerful American guys
Fond memories for me,
When I think of those GIs

My work a pleasure,
Treated with great respect,
With a 'ding' on my ticket machine
Their fares I'd collect.

So courteous, so cheerful,
The future so bleak,
Many of those soldiers
Moved on in a week.

So charming in manner
Any girl could not resent,-
The offer of those coveted nylons
As a little present.

The Castle still stands
Proud, bursting with knowledge,
Now serving the world,
As Atlantic International College.

When I pass that way
Fond memories I recall-
Of those American soldiers
And that lovely castle, behind a wall.

The castle and its estate were bought by M. Antonin Besse in 1960 and donated to the founding committee of Atlantic College. The place now receives students from all over the world and the air strip is now the soccer and rugby field for the school.

Marcross Decoy 'Q' Site, and Airfield, Grid Reference SS 935700

This decoy was initiated in early 1940 and was to do its job of drawing enemy bombing from its parent, RAF Llandow, and to a lesser extent from the adjacent station of RAF St Athan. Many incendiaries had been diverted by this Government acquisition of several fields, where hedges, fences and any other obstructions were removed to form a substantial area for the insertion of flarepaths – laying cables, and constructing a semi-underground control and electric generator building in the north-west corner. A dummy hangar was built with scaffolding poles and sheets of canvas, with drums of flammable liquids arranged about the corners, which when lit would give the appearance of an airfield.

This place had a use other than a 'Q' site, and indeed there is a document of MOD origin that refers to Marcross Airfield and this is how that came about.

The Spitfires of No.53 Operational Training Unit at nearby Llandow – who also supplied the personnel to run the 'Q' site – were to be seen each day dogfighting or formation flying in the skies around here. It was usual to pair off two Spitfires to engage one another in combat over the field and general area along the coast and they were known to use the field to put down in, in an emergency.

A sad day occurred when two pilots from No.53 OTU were skirmishing over the field and touched wing tips. The Spitfire R54382, piloted by Canadian M.A. Plomteaux, flicked into a spin, recovered, only to flick into a spin moments later and dive into the airfield of Marcross below, bursting into flames and entering the soil to some depth, witnessed by his recent partner in the air and by farm workers. The MOD report on this accident refers to the location of the accident as Marcross Airfield and the time as 15:30, 10 July 1941 and, of course, that it resulted in the loss of the pilot. The exact spot where this crash occurred can be traced by the fact that no crops can prosper on a circle of weed and scrub, no doubt due to the engine oil, fuel and hydraulic oil.

The 'Q' site had lost its purpose by 1943 and was left after clearing the field of the equipment of deceit, leaving this substantial area of grass to lead another life, a year or so later, as an occasional landing ground for the US Army encamped at St Donats Castle. While they had the King George's Field for the L4 Cubs of the artillery units based there it seems probable that the field at Marcross, a mile to the north of the camp, would have played its part as the landing ground of the divisional liaison aircraft of larger size and air ambulance types for the convalescents. As always when researching the temporary occupation of US units, in their gypsy-like movements about South Wales in the run up to the landings in Normandy, it is difficult to get confirmation of the use of the field, as most of the local men were away in the forces themselves and there were not many people alive today in the area that would have been old enough at the time to witness the occasional aircraft movements. We do have evidence from Mr David Lewis who was an evacuee from the bombing in London who had arrived in the Vale of Glamorgan and never returned from South Wales. He told me about the days of his early teens when he and his friends would cycle to vantage points at Llandow, St Athan, Rhoose, St Brides and Marcross in the period 1944–45 to gain sights of aircraft. He saw them at Marcross in the spring and summer of 1944, though only rarely. This gentleman was, forty years later, to become a workmate of mine.

The Q-site command and generator building in a corner of the road, and airfield in 2000. (Ivor Jones)

Marcross Airfield and one-time Q-site looking south from the northern extremity of the field in 2000. The clump of rough weed in the middle is – as I have been told – the place of the crash site. St Donats Castle and the US Army Camp are over to the far left of shot. (Ivor Jones)

Vale of Glamorgan showing St Donats on the coast and St Brides is also near to the Bristol Channel. St Athan is to the east and Llandow is in the centre. This was taken in 1946. (Welsh Assembly Archive)

TWENTY-TWO

Cubstrip at Hirwaun

Grid Reference SN 955052, on the south side of A465, 3 miles north-west of Aberdare

This field was close to the southern limits of town and just a mile from the slopes of some very high hills further south. It was just another in the ring of cubstrips that encircled the artillery ranges of the Mynedd Epynt and other ranges in the middle of Wales.

The artillery battalions of each division had little practice before leaving the US for the UK, especially in air to ground liaison. The Cubs and their pilots flew from an amazing assortment of places – roads, airfields, farm fields, village greens, golf courses, soccer pitches, parks and commons. In this part of Wales there were the ranges and the spaces to land, but the need was such that many of the units that had spent some time at the ranges were sent packing to enable another unit to have a turn.

This field was used by the 322nd Field Artillery Battalion of the 83rd Infantry Division US Army from late 1943 to May 1944 and is now the Recreation Grounds of Hirwaun Council, with a fine soccer pitch and tennis courts.

This is the airfield today at Hirwaun. There was a considerable space between the cubstrip and the town in the 1940s, but the town has built southward to meet the old site. (Ivor Jones)

A slightly blurred view over the town of Hirwaun on 14 January 1946 and the field chosen by the American Army for its landing ground. The ground south of the town looks rough because it was not agriculture that prevailed here, but coal. The old Tower Colliery was at the south of the cubstrip. (Welsh Assembly Government Photographic Archive)

TWENTY-THREE

St Bride's Satellite Landing Ground

Grid Reference SS 900735, No.6 Satellite Landing Ground on both sides of B4265, South Glamorgan

This site was first inspected on 15 December 1940. Photographic Reconnaissance Unit sorties surveyed many sites along this part of the coast on 8 September 1940. The fields that were chosen were not the best with regard to flatness – there were far better a little east along the coast – but they did have good access and, more importantly, plenty of woods to hide the aircraft. The SLG was to serve No.19 MU at St Athan.

The land belonged to the Earl of Dunraven, whose castle was on the cliffs to the south of the SLG. These lands were primarily the acreage of Pitcot Farm on the south side of B4265, with Penuchadre Farm to the north of the road. Trees were felled, hedges ripped out and gates installed, connecting the landing strips with each other across the road. Concrete bridges were built over streams enabling the aircraft to move across to fields further away.

A Robin hangar was erected with a large concrete apron sometime late in the war – believed to be 1944 – 400 yards south-west from the road. This is served by a narrow track that has the site office in a bungalow at the junction of track and B4265. A Blister hangar was built near Pitcot Farm and small Nashcrete building erected near Penuchadre Farm to act as a canteen and shelter from the worst of the weather.

I have spoken to a few of the villagers of St Brides who are of an age to remember the period and all say that the landings and take-offs were, in the end, confined totally to the MU's pilots who had experience of the two strips' idiosyncrasies. Mr William Morgan, who worked on Penuchadre Farm during the war and was close to the airmen at the SLG, said:

> Sometimes the N.W. to S.E. strip at Penuchadre was the duty strip but usually the N.E. to S.W. strip on the south of the B4265 [was] most in use. It was not only the wind direction that dictated this, but also the state of the ground and whether flooding was apparent. The aircraft type that was being delivered, also had a bearing on which to use. There were 55 aircraft in store here in June 1943.

Mr Morgan said that the fields to the north had aircraft tucked away in the woods, behind walls and under nets and they stayed for a long time at the site. He also claims that aircraft were delivered in crates by road. There were aero-engine fitters, both RAF and civvies, changing engines and assembling aircraft.

No.6 Satellite Landing Ground (SLG) in the village of St Brides on 24 April 1942.
The aircraft stored that are visible are ringed, but there are many more hidden.
The office at the top right is extant but hidden by growth. The Robin hangar and
concrete apron can be seen at the lower middle of the picture. (Welsh Assembly
Government Photographic Archive)

The north–south
airstrip, looking
southward to the sea.
The photograph was
taken in 2000 on the
B4265 road, and the
woods to the left are
part of the forest that
concealed most of the
aircraft placed in care
here. (Ivor Jones)

The large area of concrete shown supported a Robin hangar and served as an apron. The telegraph poles served telephones in the office and also the hangar. The poles follow the line of the narrow road from here to the office and the B4265. The concealment woods are to the right. (Ivor Jones)

This is the north-west to south-east runway looking to the south-east, with the B4265 on the right. (Ivor Jones)

The office and HQ of No.6 SLG with the initial telegraph pole of the site, in front of the building, on the edge of the B4265 in 2000. (Ivor Jones)

This super oblique shows Dunraven Castle and the SLG above it on 7 August 1959. I have added the lines of aircraft approach for both airstrips and the line of the road. The lovely beach at Southern Down is to be seen at the bottom left. (Welsh Assembly Government Archive)

An extract from *A History of St Brides Parish* by Mr S.W. Bevan, written in 1980 and published by D. Brown & Sons, Cowbridge, states:

> ... during the latter part of the war the parish became a declared military area with the Pitcot end of the village becoming a satellite airfield with air force personnel from RAF, Australian and New Zealand Air forces.

I was fortunate to make contact with Mr David Pearce of Bridgend who was an Air Training Corps NCO during the period until he joined the RAF as aircrew in 1945. David lived a couple of fields away at Southerndown and, together with his friends who were also ATC lads, would go to the SLG boundary fences and study the traffic on the site. After a friendship developed between the airmen working on the site and these lads, they were allowed in to do jobs such as clean up oil drip trays, and polish up the Perspex windscreens. David says that it was probably April or May of 1941 before the first of a steady trickle of aircraft arrived. Hurricane 1s were the type that first flew in. Spitfires were not stored in any quantity here, as the parent No.19 MU ferry pilots thought the landing speed of that aircraft was wrong for the undulating surface. As if to emphasise this, on June 10 1942, a No.53 OTU Spitfire from Llandow attempted to make a forced landing on the north-west to south-east strip and came to grief doing it.

David believes that it was the Beaufighters that predominated here with all marks represented: Hercules engines, Merlin engines, Fighters and Night Fighters. There were plenty of Hurricanes, Mustangs, Blackburn Bothas, Defiants and Henleys. One surprise that he witnessed was the only nose-wheel landing there, when a black Boston/Havoc came in over the sea, past the castle and landed on the southern strip. It was only a visitor! They identified a wheeled Kingfisher and witnessed the landing of the only bi-plane there, an Audax. He remembers a row of Bothas lining the hedge at Penuchadre Farm along the road. He also remembers, in the run up to D-Day, how frantic the comings and goings were at St Brides and how in the spring of 1945 the field to the rear of Pitcot Farm was full of Mustang IVs. David thought they were being accumulated for the coming Japanese battle. A lot of time expired and Hawker Henleys were scrapped here, along with a few Beaufighters.

The overhead RAF photograph below shows Beaufighters hiding in the trees and other types shoved into hedges. The oblique gives a perspective of the area concerned and the approximate number of the landing runs. It also shows how extensive the woods are and why the site was chosen. There were eighty plus aircraft held in 1944.

The SLG closed down in July 1945 as far as the Royal Air Force was concerned, but a working party from the Bristol Aero Co. stayed on to finish off the eighteen outstanding Beaufighters 1s and a few Henleys, closing down altogether on 26 September 1945. All the ground was de-requisitioned then and, as now, is under the plough.

The base of the Robin hangar is still there and the ruins of the site office/cottage. The telephone system poles run along the track to the Robin hangar and stop dead there. The evidence of gully bridging and gate erection is evident where none is currently needed.

This picture is of interest for two reasons: flying over the SLG at St Brides, someone has made the effort to ink in what was on the ground below the plane, and the aircraft is Miles Martinet P428, on the strength of No.7 Gunnery school, at nearby RAF Stormy Down. Note the aircraft stored in the tree line. This was 1943. (Phillip Davies)

TWENTY-FOUR

Airstrips at the Sennybridge Ranges

Grid References of the airstrips: Drovers Arms SN 975 450; Tirabad SN 880 415; Clawdd SN 870 380; US Army Cubstrip SN 915 280

Sennybridge lies on the A40 Brecon to Llandovery road and the Army's artillery ranges lie to the north of this small town. The training area covers approximately 37,000 acres and consists of various types of terrain. A large part is upland moor, known as Mynedd Epynt, which ranges in height from 300–475m. The impact area of 14,000 acres is located here. The remainder of this modern training area consists of rural farmland and coniferous forest, some of which is leased from the Forestry Commision.

With the outbreak of war in 1939 the requirement for military training grounds increased and Mynedd Epynt was chosen as an artillery range. Requisition orders were issued giving the local population until April 1940 to move out. This was then extended to June, by which time it was declared clear. A total of fifty-four dwellings and 219 people had been evacuated.

Sennybridge's earliest use was for artillery only training. This consisted of Fire & Movement practice for Field, Medium, and Heavy Units of the Allied Forces. On 22 May 1940, No.6 Practice Camp Battery, Royal Artillery, was formed here and many nationalities used its facilities, including American, Canadian and Czech.

German and Italian POWs were put to work building roads, buildings, water and supply dumps all over this large site that extended north from the A40 to Llangammerch Wells, east to the Brecon to Builth road (B4520) and west to the Crychan Forest and A483.

By 1943 the emphasis was on anti-tank training. The enemy's tanks were destroying ours at a ratio of three to one. They had better armour and better guns; we had to catch up. Techniques of anti-tank warfare from the air and ground were developed here. This was a case of what Castlemartin was to tank warfare training, Sennybridge was to anti-tank warfare.

At the end of the war other training, such as small arms, mortars and airborne, parachute and SAS commando training exercises, took up the ranges and in 1960 it was renamed All Arms Training Area. Its present name is Sennybridge Training Area, with four Ministry of Defence units. The Sennybridge Training Unit is the major one and is the host to the others: a detachment of No.39 District Workshops, Royal Electrical & Mechanical Engineers, a detachment of No.241 Signals Squadron and a Transport & Material Park, Royal Army Ordnance Corps. The host is responsible for accommodating,

Sennybridge Camp on 4 May 1946, also showing the US Army Piper Cub field to the south of the A40, with the river Usk circling it on the southern side. This field was used by many units of the army artillery's L4 AOPs (Air Observation Post Piper Cubs). (Welsh Assembly Government Photographic Archive)

Churchill tank target for air to ground attack training at Sennybridge. (Mark Khan)

feeding and fuelling visiting units undergoing instruction, which may be of battalion (infantry) 650-man strength or of platoon forty-man strength.

Aviation at Sennybridge
Light fixed wing aircraft abounded on these ranges during the war – Austers, Beavers, Piper Cubs, Stinson Sentinels and Lysanders – and there were four airstrips to

The Helicopter pads at the camp. Two Pumas disgorge attacking troops in an exercise in March 2004. (Ivor Jones)

This is the famous onetime public house, the Drovers Arms, now a shelter for troops on the top of the mountain. The airstrips named after this former pub are some 300m to the south-west of here. March 2000. (Ivor Jones)

accommodate them, acting in the Air Observation Post (AOP) role. There were also more aggressive roles to be played in the air at the ranges: anti-tank cannon fire, rockets, missiles and bombs. In Ground attack exercises with troops, troops supply drops, parachute drops, simulated attacks on prepared infantry or artillery positions and support of an attack.

The main landing ground is named Clawdd, because of its proximity to an old British camp. There have been no fixed wing aircraft movements from here since the 1980s, only helicopter. It is a small field of grass that was used briefly for incinerating the animals slaughtered during the foot and mouth outbreak. It has been cleaned up, extended, graded, and compacted, with a view to using the C130 Hercules on this field.

The airstrip furthest north is the Drovers Arms, so named because it is near an old inn of that name that no longer gives shelter and comfort to the public but is now a shelter for troops on the far ranges. Remarkably, this inn was famous in the past for being a stopping place on the long cattle and sheep drives from mid-Wales to the markets of London. Near the inn is the mountain, Drum Ddu, and the airstrip was carved out of

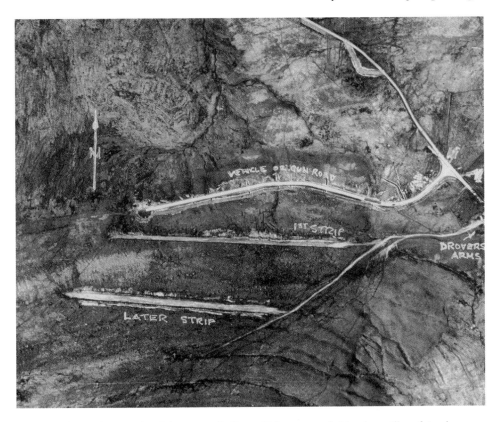

Stood on the north-east side of the mountain Drum Ddu, surrounded by the artillery firing bases, were the AOP airstrips of Drovers Arms. (Welsh Assembly Government Photographic Archive)

its north-east side at an elevation of 441m. Shrouded frequently in hill fog and exposed to hostile weather, it was in use throughout the war.

Over to the west, at Llandulas, is the airstrip of Tirabad. This was made with two runways forming a cross, with all four ends being somewhat lower than the centre, and was not popular with the pilots as they could never see over the crest when taking off or landing.

The fourth airstrip was acquired by the US Army for their Piper Cub L4s when using the ranges for artillery practice. The difference with this strip is that it was outside the enclosed facility at Epynt. It was located half a mile west of the town of Sennybridge, south of A40 and alongside the river Usk. The unit most identified with this strip was the 250th Field Artillery Battalion, but other US Army units used it when attending courses on the ranges.

All of these strips are disused now except that of Clawdd, which although not used by the military since the advent of the helicopter – they land anywhere – has seen a few jobs come its way, such as the television company that made a film about the Falklands War here in 1984, with mock ups of Pucara aircraft being bombed and blown up in spectacular fashion. Before that 1980 was the last time a fixed wing landing was made, and this was by the firm spraying the bracken on the ranges – a private single seater.

The following aircraft types were used at Sennybridge over the years, although obviously the jets and large aircraft were not landing or taking off from here but were

Above left: About halfway along the Drovers Arms airstrip. (Ivor Jones)

Above right: The western end of the Drovers airstrip. Little used now but British Army Austers were using the strip during the war. (Ivor Jones)

Looking east from mid-airfield at Tirabad in March 2004. (Ivor Jones)

operating from other bases: Auster, Cub, Beaver, Hurricane 11c, Typhoon, Hunter, Hawk, A10 Thunderbolt, Tornado, Harrier, Jaguar, Jet Provost, Vampire, Javelin, Meteor, Argosy, Beverly, Hastings and Hercules. The following types of helicopters were used: Sioux, Alouette, Gazelle, Wessex, Puma, Lynx, Chinook and CH53 Jolly Green Giant.

There are two parachute dropping zones, a personnel drop zone (DZA) and a heavy supply drop zone (DZB). The former of 340 acres and the latter 350 acres, these are in the southern area of the training site.

The helicopter is an everyday sight here, lifting guns and vehicles and simulating casualty evacuation. This has an intrusive noise nuisance effect on the whole base and ways of minimising this are being sought. It is the ground attack practice with helicopters that shows how effective they can be. A live firing range was established at a point in the range, named Mabioin Way, in 1977. The range provided a flight path from which the helicopter could safely fire automatic fire into a marked area stretching from Bryn Du to Gallows Hill. The first unit to use it was an American helicopter squadron working with No.38 Group RAF. The aircraft used were the CH 53s (Jolly Green Giants) which were truly formidable, delivering a saturating volume of firepower into the target. British helicopter units use the range, including squadrons of the Fleet Air Arm whose role was ground strike using carrier based aircraft.

The most concentrated period of helicopter use was during the preparations for the Falklands War in 1982 when a whole Infantry Brigade with all its supporting arms were

The long disused airfield at Tirabad. The grass runways formed a cross and I have marked them to show the location as described to me. Surrounded by rifle ranges and artillery firing platforms, Austers and Beavers, plus the Cubs, flew off it the until the mid-1950s. In its early days it was known as the Llandulas Strip. (Welsh Assembly Government Photographic Archive)

Looking south at Tirabad from mid-airfield. Note how the ground falls away in each direction. The centre of the airfield is at the highest ground. (Ivor Jones)

This is the largest airfield at Sennybridge, named Clawdd. Looking north-east to the start of the runway in March 2004, we are roughly at the middle of its length. (Ivor Jones)

Left: Looking across the runway at Clawdd at its widest and about midway down its stretch. This was used for the mass cremation of cattle during the BSE outbreak, but there are now plans to extend the airfield to accommodate the Hercules transport aircraft. (Ivor Jones)

Left: This picture shows GIs struggling with skis for the Cubs, possibly at Sennybridge. (Ken Wakefield)

Below: A view from the A40 of the cubfield used by units of the US Army during 1943–1945. The river Usk is at the tree line.

air lifted from Sennybridge Camp to the Training Area. The noise of the 'choppers' was the talk of the village, but nobody complained because the exercise was so essential to ensure there would be no disasters later in the South Atlantic.

At this time there is a commonality in training and tactics between all three services, under the cover of the Ministry of Defence.

I was fortunate in getting a favourable reply to my request for admission onto the ranges. On the day of my arranged visit there was no firing expected in the areas I wished to see, but unfortunately for me it had snowed during the previous forty-eight hours and the mountains were covered. I was driven from one to the other of the airstrips in a four-wheel-drive Land Rover but we still slid on the slopes that failed to face the sun. Not only that, it was hopeless for photographing grass strips on the high altitude snow-covered grass, it was difficult to locate them. Luckily my driver, ex-Sergeant Major David Muirhead, was an old hand on the ranges and due to the huge distances between the airstrips – I had assumed prior to this that a couple of hours would do – we were out for four hours. The views from the high points are stunning and it is possible to visit the periphery of the ranges on public roads that still provide these views, except when the red flag is flying near the impact areas.

TWENTY-FIVE

Airstrip at Pen-y-Waun Farm, near Babel

5 miles north-east of Llandovery, Carmarthenshire

This was another of the fields requisitioned by the US Army for their Piper Cub L4s for the period before the D-Day landings in France. Each of the field artillery battalions needed a field near the ranges for the necessary practice of air to ground radio instruction between the Air Observation Post who spotted fall of shot and the batteries on the ground who made the necessary adjustments to the artillery.

The farmer at Pen-y-Waun Farm had a visit from an army representative and the next day the aircraft flew in and the tents were erected. For an unknown period of time this unknown unit operated from this very remote place situated on the south-western limits of the Mynedd Epynt range.

Mr Jim Davies answered an advertisement I placed in the local paper referring to the cubstrip at Llandovery. Jim confirmed what was needed for Llandovery and stressed the need to research this field, previously unheard of in Pentre-Ty-Gwyn or, more precisely, Babel. Jim was brought up on a nearby farm, Efail Fach, and was daily able to see the routine of this tented camp and be thrilled by the presence of the Piper Cubs. Aircraft were rarely seen in this neck of the woods in 1943–44 and he remembers the hustle and bustle of the Dodge 1½ ton 6x6 trucks, ¾ ton 4x4 weapons carriers and, of course, the ubiquitous jeeps rushing along the country roads that had never seen anything like it before.

Not all of the American units using airstrips in the mountains of southern mid-Wales were attending exercises on the Sennybridge complex of ranges. There was another to the north-west of this named the Llangurig (Cambrian) Battle School, an area of hills, valleys and marshes that extended over a vast area of land commandeered to practise under the battle conditions that would be met on the Continent. Used mostly by armoured divisions, they still needed the cubstrips for Air Observation Post L4s and many of the fields in this book served the Battle School.

The US Army airstrip at Pen-y-Waun Farm, near Babel. This overhead shows exactly the remoteness of this camp. The main reason for its use was simply because it lies just on the south-west limits of the Sennybridge Ranges which the American artillery units were desperate to get time in. Taken on 27 August 1945, a year after the last of them had evacuated this quiet and lovely place. (Welsh Assembly Government Photographic Archive)

Left: The field, used by the Piper Cub L4 AOP aircraft, is the far one on this photograph taken from the front of the farmhouse, Pen-y-Waun, looking to the south west. (Ivor Jones)

Below: The cubfield at Pen-y-Waun Farm. (Ivor Jones)

TWENTY-SIX

Airstrip at Island Farm Camp

On A48, south of Bridgend

This is a large sprawling area of prefabricated concrete huts arranged around catering, ablution, and entertainment buildings built in red brick, with a parade ground and football pitch. It was all built on rising ground, which fuels speculation that in the distant past the place may have been the only land not flooded for periods.

The camp was initially built for accommodating many hundreds of women workers at the newly built Royal Ordnance Factory, but this was not taken up by the ladies, who preferred to return home after each shift, as transport to the surrounding towns and villages was good.

The camp was left empty for the most part until the arrival of the US Army in the UK. There was a concentration of divisions and brigades along the ports of South Wales and in the case of Island Farm Camp it received, at some point, the 12th Field Artillery Battalion of the US Army. This raised the need for an airstrip as near as possible to the camp to accommodate the two Piper L4 Air Observation Post aircraft that the battalion used for spotting fall of shot for the artillery and communications.

No one seems to be able to point out for sure which of the surrounding fields filled the needs of the L4s, but it pretty well solves the question when one looks around this area, as the alternatives have hazards or deficiencies that must have been there in 1943. There is a path that is still discernable from the camp to a gap in the hedges of the airfield. The field is large enough and square to suit most wind conditions. Grid reference SS 899781.

When the Americans moved on in 1944, it coincided with a need for more prisoner of war cages. The men captured in the closing stages of the North African, Italian and French campaigns had surprised the Allies by their numbers, so Island Farm Camp became POW Camp 198.

The history of the POW camp is not relevant to this airstrip but it must be said that the place became famous for having the biggest escape breakout of POWs ever, mostly due to deplorable security. After digging two tunnels, sixty-six men escaped on the night of 10–11 March 1945, from hut No.9 where the tunnels started. After many adventures and great distances covered by some, they were all rounded up. An inquest into the affair decided that lax security was to blame and all the prisoners were sent elsewhere. By 31 March 1945 it was emptied of the rank and file that had comprised the population of Camp 198 and it became No.11 (Special) Camp.

Island Farm Camp. This overhead shows the camp and the airstrip, which was to the south. Dated 4 December 1946, it was still holding POWs. (Welsh Assembly Government Photographic Archive)

Looking south-west to the limits at the corner of the airfield at Island Farm in 2003. (Ivor Jones)

This montage of 2003 is an attempt to show the size of the airstrip at Island Farm. The camp buildings begin at far right. (Ivor Jones)

This is the last of the camp buildings at Island Farm in 2004. It has been refurbished at considerable expense because it is, I believe, the hut from which the escape of German prisoners occurred. It is now something of a museum. (Ivor Jones)

During the six years of war the allies had captured many senior Axis officers who were encamped at various places and in early January 1946, 127 officers of general or equivalent rank were transferred here, including four field marshals, von Runstedt, von Kleist, von Brauchitsch and von Manstein, and many other well-known names.

By May 1948 the camp had removed the prisoners back to Germany and the place was officially closed. The camp stayed exactly as it was for fifty years, except for the use by the Territorial Army of one of the buildings as a meeting place, but the whole site has now been reduced to rubble, except for just one refurbished accommodation block, conserved for posterity.

TWENTY-SEVEN

RAF Stormy Down

Grid Reference SS 840795, Mid Glamorgan

In 1934 rumours of a bombing range at Margam Sands and a bombing school to be built on the hill known as Newton Down were rife. The plateau was of solid limestone, and large quarries surrounded the site where the airfield was to be built.

However, it was to be a long wait for the rumours to bear fruit. Work started in March 1938. The main contractor was Garrard & Sons of Manchester and the original estimate £180,000, but by the time the base opened £210,000 had been spent, with a further £70,000 needed to complete the hutted camp. The only brick buildings were for the station CO and the senior medical officer and married quarters for two warrant officers and fourteen airmen, who had to be at least twenty-six years of age.

No.9 Armament Training Station formed here on 24 April 1939 on what was then RAF Newton Down. Both the school and the station were to change names shortly after. Administered by No.25 Armament Training Group in Training Command, the CO was Wg Cdr S.C.P. Wood who, only a week after the opening, handed over to Wg Cdr T.O. Clougston. The total strength was nine officers and 180 airmen.

RAF Newton Down was re-named RAF Porthcawl soon after its commissioning as it was causing confusion with another station in Nottinghamshire (Newton). It was used by pilot pupils from the affiliated Flying Training Schools for three weeks' air firing and bombing practice, in the manner of the later Armament Practice Camps.

The syllabus included air to air and air to ground combat, and bombing with 10lb smoke bombs from a high level in which grouping and accuracy were tested. There were also low-level attacks. The unit was flying Henley 111s.

The air to ground firing was carried out along Sker beach and Margam Sands on either side of the estuary of the river Kenfig. The range consisted of four 10ft sq. screen targets, situated north to south from Margam to Sker, with roman numerals marked one to four set out on the edge of the dunes. When the tide was out eight fabric targets were laid out on the beach instead. A further four portable targets, marked A to D, were set on the beach for grouping practice.

Conical sleeves were towed by aircraft, initially six Hawker Henleys, for air to air firing over the sea. Offshore, the outer limits were marked by five buoys and a pyramidal reinforced large raft was used as a bombing target.

On the Southerndown side of Porthcawl was another tow-line, 100 yards from the shore, running from Tusker Rock to Nash Point, for use by day at altitudes of 1,000–1,500ft. Further out, and parallel to the inshore line, was a tow-line 1½ miles out to sea to be flown at 4,000–5,000ft. Further out still into the Bristol Channel was a target area

Former RAF Stormy Down on 4 December 1946 after its closure as an operational training base though many were to use its accommodation huts in the coming years. Note the four Blister hangars at the bottom right of the picture – these are the hangars used for the US Army Piper Cubs' maintenance. (Welsh Assembly Government Photographic Archive)

This Avro Anson with No.7 Air Gunnery School, Stormy Down, has a turret fitted for the student gunners, and not the standard one. The instructors' viewing cupola is near the radio mast.

RAF Stormy Down's accommodation and technical sites. (Welsh Assembly Government Photographic Archive)

Hawker Henley target-towing aircraft were used after the Wallaces, and then the Battles, had been retired. Even these were replaced by the Defiant and, later, the Miles Martinet before the war's end.

measuring 3 x 5 miles. At sea, down channel, were three more target practice areas and the Tusker Rock itself was used.

The first of the pilot training school to arrive was the advanced training squadron of No.5 FTS (Flying Training School) from Sealand.

The organisation consisted of Station HQ, Station Flights Workshops, Armament Section and the Marine Craft Section based at Porthcawl Harbour. The latter consisted

Air–sea rescue
boats of the
Marine Craft
Section on the
strength of the
Air Observer
School
and No.7
Bombing
and Gunnery
School at
Stormy Down.
(F. Jones)

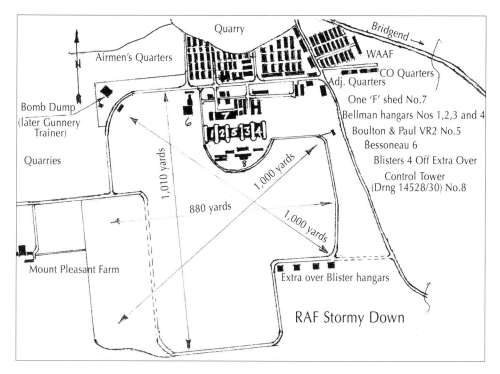

This map is to enable the reader to understand how small – and inadequate – the landing area at
Stormy Down was. When one adds that it was pot-holed, as well as poorly drained, one can really
sympathise with the young men who flew from this airfield. (Drawing by Ivor Jones)

of two armoured target boats, A569 and A571. There were also three sea-tenders for use
as crash and safety boats.

On 1 September 1939, two days before war was declared, No.9 Armament Training
Station was disbanded to become No.7 Air Observers School with a new establishment,
and on the day war was declared ten Wallaces and six Henleys arrived from No.1 Air
Observers School at North Fitties, with nine officers and thirty-nine other ranks.

The Westland Wallace was the aircraft type first used as a target tug at Stormy Down. The writer, as a lad of twelve years, was helped into the cockpit of one at an open day at Stormy Down in about 1940. (F. Jones)

On Tuesday 5 September four Fairy Battles were received from No.8 MU at Little Rissington. Two weeks later No.7 AOS collected the first HP Harrow No.K7014 from No. 6 MU, Brize Norton.

On Monday 11 September sixty airmen wireless operators from No.2 Electrical and Wireless School, Yatesbury, arrived at Porthcawl to form No.1 Air Gunners Course, for training that would take four weeks.

The first Air Observer Course began on 16 October 1939. Eight weeks later, twenty-seven had passed and two were given further instruction. The teaching had included course setting, bomb sight and practice on the AML Bombing Teacher on the ground. Practical elements included bombing from four directions, using the camera obscura or track recorder, bomb dropping on stationary targets, moving targets (the armoured boats) and low-level bombing. Observers also did the Gunnery Course, which was twelve hours long, compared with the Air Gunners' eighteen hours.

On 20 October a detachment from No.2 Flying Training School arrived with nine Oxfords and ten Harvards. Thirty-seven of the aircrew officers were billeted in the Seabank Hotel in Porthcawl.

On Sunday 19 November there was a foretaste of the trouble that was to dog this airfield – bad ground. An Oxford L4632 wrecked its undercarriage when the surface of turf concealed a hole in the limestone and a wheel fell into the subsidence. A lodger unit, No.14 OTU, wrote off one of its Hampdens when its undercarriage collapsed.

The first Whitley, K7212, arrived on 25 November 1939 from No.166 Squadron, soon to be followed by two more, plus three Battles, nine Harrows, twelve Henleys, one Magister, four Whitleys and nine Wallaces.

The station was renamed again and was henceforth to be known as Stormy Down. Some people thought this was in reference to the weather, but this was not so. The new name was, in fact, a reference to Sturmi, the medieval lord who had his castle and land nearby.

Whitley Mk 1 of No.7 Bombing & Gunnery School at Stormy Down. (F. Jones)

The Air Observer and the Air Gunner Courses continued to turn out successful pupils. The 5th Air Observation course delivered twenty-one observers in April 1940 at the end of their ten weeks, during which time they had flown an average of 32 hours and 18 minutes, fired 2,061 rounds, shot off three rolls of camera gun film and dropped fifty bombs. A new directive gave priority to high-level bombing; low-level bombing was no longer an advanced subject on the course.

Of the air gunners in their four weeks of training, fifty passed the course, flying an average of 13 hours and 45 minutes. They fired 2,038 rounds and 6.3 camera gun films.

During May 1940 two more seaplane tenders arrived at the marine section at Porthcawl harbour, Nos 294 and 295.

On the 20 June 1940 No.2 Air Armament School (AAS) moved in from Pembrey. With their arrival the ration strength rose to 1,469. No.2 AAS included six Fitter-Armourer Direct Entry Courses. In addition to the direct entry fitters there were eleven courses from armourer to fitter and three Naval Air Mechanic (Observer) Courses, undergoing 16 weeks of ground element in their training. This unit was disbanded here on 20 June 1940 to become No.3 Ground Armament School.

On 10 July 1940, during yet another air-raid alert, the CO, Flying Wg Cdr Ira Jones, who had had forty kills in the First World War and was a very patriotic Welshman, spotted a German aircraft across the bay over Swansea. He leapt into a Hawker Henley and sped off in pursuit. Diving out of the sun onto the Ju 88, he fired his only weapon, a Very signal pistol, before turning into clouds. The enemy gunner opened fire and hit the Henley's port wing. It made a dodgy landing back at base after developing tail flutter.

17 July saw the arrival of Flt Lt S.E. Pritchard and five other officers from the Central Flying School, who had qualified on No.5 War (Flying Instructors') Course. They were to give refresher and night flying training to officers. Setting out in April 1940, with three Battle Trainers, they visited all No.25 Group flying stations – Evanton, West Freugh, Aldergrove, Jurby, Penhros, Stormy, Warmwell, Manby and Pembrey – spending a week at each.

Sker House near the beach. During the war it housed the Range Party whose task was to recover the dropped target drogues, or socks. The field facing the house was the drop zone. This house has been the subject of many tales of smuggling and drama since the seventeenth century. (Ivor Jones)

The station complement at this time was forty-two officers, eighty-eight NCOs and 1,020 airmen and sailors. Four more Whitleys were added to the establishment of twenty, plus sixteen Battles. On 27 July 1940, the day No.17 Air Gunnery Course passed out, a Fairy Battle was lost at sea. Flying Officer Wheeler was on gunnery training when he made a forced landing off Porthcawl. The aircraft sank in 75 seconds, taking the pilot and pupils Cpl Barringer and AC2 Barker with it.

That same day Pilot Officer Swyers landed Henley L3362 after the weather test and taxied into the fire tender. 19 July saw Wallace K5078 severely damaged when Sgt Price, making a forced landing in a field at Wick, undershot and crashed into a hedge.

In August, there were four accidents involving aircraft of No.1 FTS on attachment here. On the 4th Hind K4652 was written-off after Leading Airman Heath stalled at 20ft and crashed onto the airfield. Hind K5471 ran into a stone, after Acting Lead Airman Langdon made a forced landing into a field, below Pencastell Farm, Kenfig Hill, on the same day.

Two days later, A/L/A Fletcher in Battle K7640 overshot on landing and ran into the hedge and on 8 August, in Battle P6737, A/L/A O'Shea made a wheels-up landing.

During August the range party out on the beach and dunes at Margam Sands moved to Sker House, where they had a drogue dropping field. Previously they were dropped on the dunes.

This airfield's turn to be bombed came on 21 August when three Ju 88s roared across the field, gunning and bombing as they went. Four bombs landed on the airfield and exploded, while another four fell among the wooden huts. Four more fell beyond the camp and did not explode. Three were blown up by armament personnel, but it was not until September 1970 that the fourth bomb was found during quarrying and was blown up by the army.

Group Captain A.W. Franklyn assumed command of No.7 BGS in October 1940 just as the autumn clouds were affecting the flying programme. The outer tow-lines were unserviceable. On the Friday there was no flying and on Saturday both the outer

The Boulton Paul Defiant Mk III target tower was used at Stormy Down by No.7 AGS.

tow-lines and the C–D Lines were washed out. That was the day the 22nd Air Gunners Course was posted to Kinloss on passing out. None of these gunners had fired on the 200 or 400 yard ground ranges, as these were still uncompleted.

Battle K7626 of No.1 FTS was damaged in a wheels-up landing but, taking advantage of a fine day, an intensive programme was flown on Friday 11 October; all ranges were used and 197 hours were flown. On the next day 163 hours were flown and on Sunday there was flying but no bombs were dropped. Weeks of low cloud would intervene with intermittent rain but, even so, flying would be attempted between those spells to keep the courses on time.

Flt Sgt Tingley landed his Battle L5688 with his gear up on the 21st and on the 29th a Polish trainee, LAC K. Dindorf, did the same. The next day Sgt T. Lambert in Whitley K9016 undershot and hit the boundary fence with his undercarriage, which then collapsed.

November 1940 began with continuous rain and flying with No.7 BGS was cancelled. All trainees spent that day and the next in lecture rooms. No.1 FTS carried on flying, only to have Hind K 6713 skid, overturn and be written off. The pilot, A/L/A McWilliams, was unhurt.

More buildings were completed and handed over to the RAF. They included technical facilities, ablutions and latrines, classrooms, offices, gun and turret buildings, workshops, camera obscura, air-raid shelters and two MG ranges. Recent courses had suffered from a shortage of reflector gun sights and cine gun film.

On 6 November 1940 Hind K6770 suffered undercarriage damage on landing. A day later, Sgt Subkowiak (Poland) taxied Whitley K7194 into a hangar stanchion when his brakes failed.

More aircraft were damaged on the 12th. Gale-force winds of up to 100mph played havoc with a Battle, two Wallaces, and three Whitleys. One Whitley was thrown right across the aerodrome.

Courses got larger and buildings at Coney Beach fairground were taken over as billets. At the beginning of December Squadron Leader Bathurst arrived from St Athan to arrange practice bombing on the range by wireless transmission controlled Queen Bee aircraft. Results were to be observed by Stormy personnel. The results were encouraging, with a bombing error of 1194ft from 10,000ft. Tests went on for the rest of the month.

Mist, rain and wind gusts were a daily feature. Returning from target-towing in Battle V1214 on Thurs 5 December 1940, Pilot Officer Davies attempted to land in 50mph gusts and undershot. The undercarriage hit the boundary bank and a wheel broke off. Neither the pilot nor the Tow operator were hurt. The next day gales reached 80mph and catching one Whitley, at piquet, the wind twisted it around until it tore the wheels off.

On New Years Eve Whitley K 8977, belonging to No.10 OTU, made a heavy landing and was damaged. It was repaired by a contractor working party from Marshalls of Cambridge and after repair was allocated to Stormy Down.

Anson LT 830 of No.7 AGS with the pupil gunner in the turret aiming at the drogue above. The instructor is standing in the cockpit observing the technique used. (RAF Stormy Down Museum)

Showing the poor vision that the controller had of aircraft movement on this south west corner of the airfield: when looking from the tower any aircraft were hidden. (Ivor Jones)

The Jennings building which was at the centre of the repair and maintenance of the many boats used by the AGS at Stormy Down. Note the slipway on the left and the harbour entrance on the right. (Ivor Jones)

This Hampden Mk 1, serial L4042, coded MG-M, was with No.7 Squadron (No.16 OTU) but on detachment to the school at Stormy Down. On 23 April 1941 it overshot the airfield because of mud, and the brakes failed to stop its momentum, passing through two hedgerows. (Phil Davies)

With a ration strength of 1,270, there was a shortage of bed space, even with the use of tents. Billets in Mary Street, Porthcawl, and at the marina base were taken over for the ninety-one incoming trainees of No.23 Air Gunnery and No.8 Observer Courses in 1941.

January brought freezing fog, but work had to continue. On the 6th there was 10/10 cloud at 1,000–2,000ft but the inner tow-lines were still run. On Tuesday 14th No.7 BGS ceased flying at 13:30, but No.1 FTS carried on even though the murk had descended to ground level. On take-off in the late afternoon, one of their Hinds collided with a parked Whitley K7196 whose starboard mainplane and spar were damaged beyond unit repair. The fate of the Hind is not recorded.

The last day of January saw further trials of the St Athan Queen Bee over the bombing range in snow showers. The snow became heavy overnight and the airfield was unusable over the weekend.

The old F-shed at Stormy Down. Once a seaplane shed on the south coast just after the First World War, it had been the major hangar here all through the Second World War and is still in use as a market place at weekends. (Ivor Jones)

At last the moving target range, with model aircraft mounted on rails, was ready. It came into use on Friday 7 February, but it was soon unserviceable again and No.30 Air Gunnery Course passed out in mid-March without ever using it.

There was a resolution as to what colour scheme to adopt for training aircraft, as target tugs were vulnerable unless coloured in high visibility, but it was decided to give all towing aircraft camouflage on their upper surfaces, to aid concealment when parked. The training Battles (bomber), Defiants and Hampdens were to be in operational colours, and Masters and Battles TT were to be in trainer colours. At the same time recognition lights were to be displayed and when within 5 miles of the aerodrome they should use navigation lights instead. No.7 BGS were issued with sets of lights for sixteen Battles (bomber), twenty-seven Battles TT and twenty-four Whitley.

The aerodrome surface was so bad that flying had to be stopped until it had dried out, as the greasy surface was rendering the aircraft's brakes worthless. On 4 March flying was stopped when it became cloudy. Later it restarted and Sgt Tock took off in Battle L5019 with LACs Staunch & Shepherd (No.30 Air Gunnery Course pupils) on quarter cross exercises. A second Battle, flown by Sgt Noble, was towing the target drogue. The two aircraft passed each other at 2,000ft and Sgt Noble saw Sgt Tock's machine turn sharply and head for Porthcawl with white smoke pouring from it. Noble turned and caught sight of Sgt Tock 500 yards away, then lost sight of him again. He did not reappear. At 13:10 a civilian reported an aircraft crashed at sea off Porthcawl, so the air-sea rescue launches left harbour but, after searching, no trace of plane or crew was found.

Trainee flight engineers now began arriving for their gunnery instruction, twenty-nine of them joining No.33 Air Gunnery Course.

On 9 June the unit became No.7 Air Gunners School (not Bombing and Gunnery School) and by the end of the month was divided into a Maintenance Wing and a Training Wing. July saw HQ Training Command's decision to stop bombing practice

The VR2 hangar with the F-shed at the rear in 2003. There were four Bellman hangars here as well, but they are long gone. The airfield watch office and traffic control were sited between this position and the VR hangars in the left-hand corner. (Ivor Jones)

at Stormy Down. In the future No.1 FTS was to fly from Netheravon using stationary targets on the Pepperpot Hill range in Wiltshire.

The armoured target boats had already left Porthcawl. In future the sea ranges were to be used only for air firing due to the formation of No.46 Air Sea Rescue Marine Craft Unit at Porthcawl on 9 September. The Marine Craft Unit was part of No.7 AGS and range facilities were disbanded.

Hurricane BD723 from Angle crashed at Stormy Down on 18 December 1941 when Flt Lt Tripe undershot and the aircraft was badly damaged (it was later repaired and sent off to Russia in April 1942). Although the first Lysander had arrived to replace Battles for target-towing, the Battles were still flying – and crashing. On 12 December Pilot Officer Ghose (Indian Air Force) made a wheels-up landing in Battle L5663. Five days later Pilot Officer Brander in Battle 5737 could not get the starboard wheel to lock down, even with the emergency gear, and made a wheels-up landing.

On the 19 September Flying Officer Jakubowsky (Poland) was on air firing detail in Whitley K7201 when the starboard engine – which worked the hydraulic pump for flaps – ran out of fuel. The fitter went to the emergency hand pump, but before he could get the gear locked down the pilot made a forced landing on the aerodrome. After running along for about 200 yards the undercarriage collapsed.

More Lysanders came for target-towing and some Defiants for gunnery training. A dual-control Magister arrived for the conversion of pilots to Defiants.

In 1942 the North Inner tow-line at 1,200ft ran from Rest Bay to Port Talbot, while the North Outer, at 3,000ft, ran parallel to it but further out. The South Inner, also at 1,200ft, ran from Newton to Nash Point, and the South Outer, at 3,000ft, again ran parallel to it but further out to sea. These were flown in a figure of eight pattern with the gunnery aircraft always on the landward side and firing out to sea. The Target Tug flew in a straight line for 6–8 minutes. There was no firing on turns because the towing aircraft and the drogue target would be in line.

The north C to D lines and south A to B lines, at 3,000ft, ran at right angles to the shore from Sker and from Ogmore-by-Sea respectively. Their position was marked by

Above: No.2 Flying Training School Airspeed Oxford had a detachment here from 20 October 1939.

Left: The last of the quadrant towers on Margam Sands. It has slid down on the sand over the last sixty years from its position on top of the dune. (Ivor Jones)

a large white arrow on the cliff tops pointing out to sea. These arrows were made of concrete poured into shuttered moulds and were 30 yards long. From these markers the tugs sometimes flew to the Somerset coast, offering a good run for firing and these were often run when the visibility was too bad for the inner and outer tow-lines.

On 13 January 1942 the first detachment from No.3 Air Observers School arrived, complete with their own Ansons for air firing. Their own airfield at Bobbington was unusable.

Almost continuous bad weather affected No.57 Air Gunnery Course whose students did not fly for a fortnight before passing out on 24 January. As a result they had had

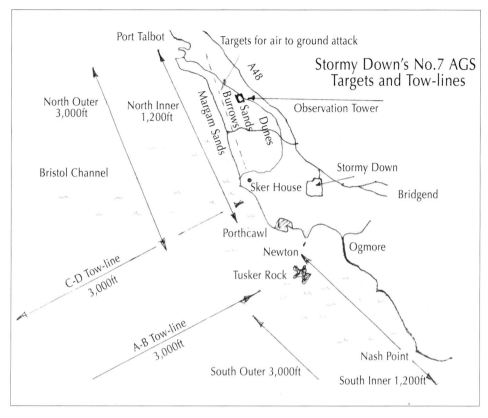

An explanation of the various target towing runs, called Tow-Lines, and also the air to ground targets. Some of these can still be seen near Port Talbot Steelworks. (Ivor Jones)

an average of only 1,041 rounds on the ground ranges at 25, 200 and 400 yards. To compensate they had each managed nearly nine hours of turret manipulation on the ground, five hours in the spotlight trainer and each pupil had fired ten shot-gun cartridges at clay pigeons.

On 31 January 1942 five more Defiants arrived from No.9 AOS Penrhos to help with the extra training load caused by the detachments from No.3 AOS. The commitment was now one course of wireless operator/air gunners, forty-five in number, and one course of forty-five air gunners a month! From 7 February this became two courses of straight air gunners, sixty a month, but included refresher courses for Empire Air Training Scheme-trained gunners.

The training programme was so far behind because of the bad weather that arrangements were made to use the runways at Llandow if Stormy became unserviceable again. Crashes on the airfield were causing concern. The bad ground was causing undercarriage failures, under shooting and over running the air field's dimensions, which meant a poor serviceability rate.

No.70 Air Gunnery Course passed out in July. Each gunner fired an average of 2,470 rounds in the air and a further 700 on the ground. Turret manipulation averaged seven hours and time spent in the spotlight trainer was six hours. A summary of flying for the July 1942 reads:

Miles Martinet target tug at Stormy Down, with No.7 AGS.

Aircraft	Strength	Serviceable	Hours flown
Whitley Mk I	7	2	82
Whitley Mk II	I	I	32
Whitley Mk III	12	4	307
Whitley Mk V	5	3	15
Lysander	25	12	678
Defiant	38	18	535
Totals	88	40	1,649

In August Flt Lt Doe arrived to discuss the proposed intake of 200 flight engineers for ground training. No.7 AGS had been upgraded to train 240 pupils. The first of the two week Flight Engineer Ground Courses started on 17 September.

During the period of April–May 1942, and a period in February 1943, Stormy Down's sea range was used for the trials of Oboe Mk 1 and Mk 2. The Beam sending stations at West Prawle and Worth Matravers in Dorset directed bombers of No.109 Squadron to the targets off Margam Sands where, on the bomb release signal from West Prawle after travelling along a line signal transmitted from Worth Matravers, the bombs were dropped. The bombers scored a fantastic hit. The quadrant towers of Margam Dunes were manned by Stormy Down observers and they could not believe that they had seen aircraft at 20,000ft in 10/10 cloud score on the target. In the February 1943 trials the US Air Force also took part with Fortresses, Liberators and Marauders. They made three trial bomb runs and somehow failed in two of them.

The new year, 1943, brought an increased training load, with a planned trainee population rising to 490. Courses now included free gunnery synthetic training. By mid-January the airfield was so sodden that flying was impossible. The Air Ministry Works Deptartment engineers from HQ Flying Training Command carried out an inspection. They found water collecting in the broken limestone rock under the top soil. After heavy rain this overflowed and soil was washed out. This created cavities under the soil which caved in when a heavy weight, such as an aeroplane, passed over. They then drew up proposals to alleviate the problem. These included parking the Defiants to

The remains of the old Armadillo shelter on the north-east side of the airfield. The armadillo was no more than an armoured lorry carrying RAF airmen to counteract a landing, or any other enemy attempt to take the airfield. It worked in liaison with the Battle HQ. (Ivor Jones)

the north-west end of the airfield and the Whitleys to the east where the ground was firmer.

When flying restarted, after three days, there was more bad news when Lysander T1588, flown by Pilot Officer K.M. Steven, was taxiing; the ground subsided and the starboard undercarriage collapsed.

During February a High frequency Direction Finding Station was set up (Oboe perhaps?). On the 3 March Pilot Officer E. Taylor (Rhodesia) was taxiing Whitley T4154 when both wheels subsided up to their axles causing severe damage. Also on the 3rd, No.1 Short Empire Air Training Gunnery Course passed out.

There were four failures out of fifty and at the end of the month the new Wireless Operator Emergency Short Ground Course started. The 25th Flight Engineer Course passed out at the end of March. They had fired 500 rounds apiece (200 in simulated night conditions) and clocked up 2 hours 38 minutes of ground turret manipulation (spotlight training).

Martinets were used first at Stormy on 5 May. Because they were so much faster than any of the previous target tugs it was decided that the firing ranges might have to be extended. By the end of the month Anson and Martinet air firing details were flying with the RAF Llandow tow-line. This extended from Nash Point to Breaksea Point further up the coast. Whitleys used the south C to D line heading out across the Bristol Channel from Ogmore. Later, because of the intensified programme, No.19 Air Firing Range on the Gower was also taken over for use by No.7 AGS.

Ansons were now used for air gunnery training and one Whitley was used to give ATC lads flying experience. All sixteen Lysanders, on strength, were replaced by eighteen Martinets. On 1 July the first accident with the Martinet occurred. Sgt E.

Guziau (Poland), taxiing in JN511, with AC Tarling as tow operator, collided with a parked Anson LT827. Just fifteen days later Sgt W. Routledge, on his third solo on type, swung on landing Martinet JN538 and the undercarriage collapsed.

In September, after an accident-free August, there were a few nasty ones. On the 19th Sgt Lovett in Anson LT831 overshot and hit the east perimeter fence. Two days later Sgt P. Strycharek (Poland) was in the circuit in Anson LT888 when Lysander T1588, piloted by Sgt W. Routledge with AC R. Tarling as tow operator, was ordered to take off. The two collided at 600ft, a quarter of a mile north-north-west of the airfield. Both crews were killed. Geoff Worley of No.117 Air Gunnery Course recalls how he flew with seventeen different pilots and carried out seven different types of exercise between 5–19 September. He flew five sorties on the 5th, three each day on the 7th, 9th, 11th and 15th, one on the 17th and another three on the 19th. He fired 200 rounds (four Vickers gas-operated drums) each on Exercise G3 (tracer demonstration), beam firing, attack tail turret and quarter crossover. He had also used 25ft of cine film. His total flying time was 16 hours and 50 minutes.

A cine camera gun flight was formed as a sub flight of Martinet pilots, specialising in attacks, with another sub flight of Anson pilots to fly cine camera gun aircraft. Soon Lieutenant D. Bordes (Free French) arrived on loan from the Central Gunnery School to instruct Martinet pilots in curve of pursuit attacks, from beam to fine quarters on the Ansons.

When the new watch office was completed, it housed the officer commanding flying, the duty pilot, airfield control and the Flying Squadron Orderly Room. Flt Lt Bear of HQ No.25 Group arrived on 11 November to re-organise the airfield control. Two weeks later preparations were made for the new system. The airfield control caravan was fitted with a radio telephone and placed at the lee end of the landing run. It took over the airfield traffic control previously exercised by a post on top of the control tower and began operating on 1 December. But, because the airfield was so convex, the caravan did not have an all-round view across the airfield, so a look-out was positioned on top of the tower to watch the blind spots. This was in RT communication with the caravan.

In November 1943 two US Army Piper Cubs were attached for hangarage and maintenance in four Blister hangars on the southern end of the field. They did not operate from here but from a strip alongside West Drive in Porthcawl. They were with the 107th Artillery Battalion.

During the first week of January 1944 two Wellingtons, with Flt Lt Lewis in charge, arrived for a five-week attachment. They were taking part in trials to see if they were more efficient for gunnery training than Ansons. The airfield was so waterlogged a week later that they were flown to Llandow where they had tarmac runways. A7AGS Martinet was detached to act as the attacking aircraft. When the trials ended they were noted as satisfactory in the end of February report.

Flying was only possible on eleven days in January. The state of the airfield was so bad that on the 8th the decision was made to take over the airfield at Rhoose as a satellite for six months. This airfield had been little used since No.53 OTU had vacated it seven months prior to its use by No.7 AGS. During this period Stormy would be kept open for visitors, servicing inspections and maintenance.

On 2 February part of the east–west runway collapsed. The airfield was completely unserviceable. An engineering inspection was carried out with a view to improving the surface and it was recommended that permanent repair be made. Whilst this work was in progress air gunner training would continue at Rhoose, so on 8 February twenty three Ansons, twenty Martinets and fifty pilots moved to Rhoose.

A visit to both Stormy Down and Rhoose by the Inspector General, ACM Sir Edgar Ludlow-Hewitt, on the 18th, was followed the next day by Air Officer Commander in Chief, Flying Training Command, Air Marshal Sir Phillip Babbington. On his return to HQ FTC it was decided that after hard standings and a concrete runway had been installed at Stormy the airfield could be reopened for full air traffic by the end of September. RAF Rhoose would then be put on a care and maintenance basis. As a first step the airfield had to be levelled and work on this started on 21 June. (However, as it happens, none of this was done. No hardstands, no runway, and certainly no levelling.) The move of staff aircrew and trainees meant there were empty huts at Stormy and all of No.7 AGS. NCOs and airmen living at the Marine Rescue base at Porthcawl harbour were moved back into camp.

The target tugs of No.587 Squadron Anti-aircraft Co-operation were also using Rhoose at this time, and congestion at vital points resulted in orders that all No.7 AGS aircraft were to have airmen at the wingtips when taxiing.

There was a change to establishment for No.7 AGS on 27 April when six Ansons were added, making twenty-seven for use and ten in reserve, plus two duel-control machines. Martinets were reduced in number by seven to total eighteen, with ten reserves. Both the Miles Master and the Tiger Moth remained, but the DH 94 was replaced by a Magister, and on 1 May three Ansons arrived from No.9 (O)AFU Penrhos to complete the strength.

Four days later No.587 Squadron, attached for target duties on Thornbury Maritime Royal Artillery School range, returned to Pengam Moors, Cardiff.

Monday 8 May was a black day for No.7 AGS, with eight deaths. Three Ansons took off from Rhoose on cine gun exercises with a Martinet. Ansons LV 300 and MG 131 collided about 1½ miles out to sea from Porthcawl Point. The duty boat put to sea only to find an empty dinghy and some wreckage. Eventually all the bodies were recovered.

Suddenly news arrived that because of the reduction in training requirements, the Air Gunners Schools were to be reorganised. No.7 was to disband by 22 September. On 2 August 1944 all aircraft returned to Stormy and preparations were made to shut down the satellite, and it was transferred to No.40 Group on 1 November. All the aircraft were serviced and prepared for allocation to new units. They were flown away by Air Transport Auxiliary pilots before 2 September. No.7 AGS was replaced briefly at Stormy by No.40 (Pilot) Initial Training Wing (ITW), which at the time was reducing its establishment from 1,150 to 850 cadets. They reformed at Stormy on 1 September but No.40 ITW itself disbanded on 27 November.

November 1944 saw the arrival at Stormy Down of a Free French contingent in the form of No.4 Aircrew Reception Centre (ACRC) and No.23 Initial Training Wing, and on 1 December the full instructional programme started with signals exercises for the wireless operator (air), flight engineer, pilot, navigator and bomb aimer cadets.

On 15 December all officers, NCOs and airmen on the strengths of No.4 ACRC and No.23 ITW were transferred to Station Headquarters, RAF Stormy Down. The total strength was now 992. The permanent staff of 542 was made up of fifty-five RAF officers, fifty-nine NCOs and 139 airmen, five WAAF officers, six WAAF NCOs and 190 airwomen. The French element was six officers, thirty NCOs and fifty-one other ranks. Trainee strength was twenty-nine cadet officers, 183 cadet NCOs and 238 airmen cadets.

Training continued until February 1946 when, on the 25th, the first party – 279 in number – left for France via Newhaven and Dieppe. They were followed on the 28th by another 279.

The RAF and WAAF element and the Initial Training Wing remained until 21 April when RAF Stormy Down closed down, leaving a care and maintenance party commanded by Flt Lt.G.H.P. Potter. All that remained was No.68 Gliding School for the Air Training Corps, which moved to St Athan in March 1947, when the care and maintenance party left.

The Airfield

This Station was always too small and cramped for the job it was asked to perform. It was perhaps adequate when operating Wallaces and Hinds, but almost suicidal when using Wellingtons, Whitleys and Hampdens. It was also too convex for safety. One can see that even today and in its position up on the plateau, just a few miles from the sea, it suffered from wet and windy weather.

It is there to be visited today, although a crop grows now on the field where the aircraft once slid and crashed, and suffered collapsed landing gear.

The Buildings

The largest hangar was the solitary 'F' Shed. It still remains, having been re-clad and is in industrial use. The VR2 type hangar also remains and has been well maintained. It is now in use as a Go Kart Club. The four Bellman hangars have been dismantled for thirty years or more. A Bessonaux hangar had been on the site, as well as four extra Over Blister hangars (Drng No.12512/41). The control tower (Drng No.14528/39) is long since demolished. There are some structures remaining, such as the Braithwaite watertank and tower (Drng No.2101/38), Air Ministry Works Department mobile plant store, an ammunition storage shelter, gun harmonisation butts and an Armadillo shelter. The moving target range, with its elaborate control linkage, can still be seen, but little else as quarrying encroaches, having already devoured all the hutted camp.

The permanent housing for married quarters for the CO and adjutant, two warrant officers and the fourteen airmen is still in use, as privately owned dwellings of course.

The Outstations

Porthcawl Harbour's slipway, buildings and moorings are a reminder of the small fleet of launches , seaplane tenders, armoured target boats and, later, air-sea rescue launches that operated from here sixty years ago. The maintenance of these and other neighbouring gunnery training units boats was done at this outer harbour, where the slipway was used to haul the craft up to be worked on at Jennings Building, which was also used as billets for the men.

Sker House was used for housing the range party, an old sixteenth-century, forbidding, isolated place and much written about in local folk tales. It was used partly because there was, and still is, a long field alongside the beach where the drogues could be dropped. This went on until August 1943, when it was decided to drop drogues on the south-east side of Stormy Airfield, where the results of the air firing could be assessed earlier.

The dunes at Margam Sands contained the quadrant and observation towers that can still be seen today. However, one does need permission from CORUS, the steel company that now owns the steelworks, as almost everything in this large area of dunes is their property now and they do enforce it. It took a lot of coaxing to get my admittance to the site. I was told that the main reason for acceding in the end was that the boss was a historian too, and was sympathetic. In the event I was successful in finding the last of the quadrant towers. In the years since the war the wind has eroded the foundations of this tower and it has slid down from its original position atop the dune into a valley where nobody goes. The original floating target was moored offshore at the point where the river Kenfig joins the sea.

7,000 air gunners completed their three seven-week courses. Earlier 400 air observers completed their courses, 2,000 flight engineers did their gunnery courses and, while they were based at St Athan's School of Technical Training, 10,000 aircrew passed through from pilots to WOP/AGS. Pilots of the Fleet Air Arm underwent the armament phase of advanced training before qualifying for their wings.

For eighteen months, from June 1940, the Ground Armament School trained 1,800 RAF and WAAF armourers, as well as several hundred sailors, destined to be telegraphist air gunners for the Fleet Air Arm.

After its short stay as a Free French air depot, this old-fashioned aerodrome, with its huts bunched up together, planned before dispersed living sites were thought of, has been very quiet indeed.

In a return visit recently I found the remains of the blockhouse that was next to the Battle HQ. The HQ has been dug up, as it lies in the middle of a farmer's crop and only the corner remains of the strong point. The guardroom at the entrance to the WAAF site is now occupied by the farmer's ponies.

TWENTY-EIGHT

Porthcawl Aerodrome

Locks Common, Mid Glamorgan

After the First World War an appetite for flying had been kindled around the whole country and some of the young pilots who had survived wanted to continue their love of flying in civilian life. Flying taxis, stunt flying and pleasure trips could make a living for some.

Porthcawl Council was approached by a Captain W. Hearne, formerly of the RFC, with a proposal to bring a flying machine to Porthcawl over the Easter holiday. He believed that it would be a good advert and he intended to establish a flying school; the town could be a second Hendon! All that he desired the town to do was provide a hangar for the machine and to give him right of monopoly, as it was most unappealing to him, when he had an aerodrome, that someone else be allowed to compete with him.

The machine was to be a DZC One and would require a hangar, 70ft x 50ft x 14ft high. The question was, could the council provide this by 10 April, the date when Capt. Hearne intended to arrive with his machine. The council decided to give him the monopoly for just one year. The council provided a marquee and told him to look for a cheap hangar.

Captain Hearne brought two Armstrong Whitworth FK3s. These were two-seat trainers G-EABY and G-EABZ registered to him on14 May 1919. He flew G-EABY to Porthcawl from Hendon via Filton, but the strange thing is he never used them at Porthcawl; instead he used Avro 504 Ks.

Both the AW FK3s were withdrawn from use in May 1920. Civil flying had not been authorised in the UK until Easter 1919.

The *Porthcawl News* said on 10 April:

> A special attraction to our town this year will be Capt. Hearne's aerial trips, which will be a great novelty to thousands of people.

Captain Hearne obtained the first license in Wales to carry passengers under license No.58, from the Air Ministry. The aerodrome – again the first in Wales – had been approved, a license granted and the two aircraft certified as airworthy. He proposed to start flying on Saturday 17 May 1919 and passenger trips would continue daily throughout the summer, weather permitting. This he did for his year of monopoly.

The brothers Holmes formed Holmes Aviation Co. Ltd in 1919 and were joined by Alan Cobham. The company later changed its title to Berkshire Aviation Co. After Alan Cobham left to work for Airco (later de Havilland), he was replaced by an experienced pilot and aero engineer, J.C.C. Taylor, who introduced wing walking to pull in the crowds.

Receiving permission to work at Porthcawl, the company was joined by O.P. Jones and A.L. Robinson. Avro 504s G-EAHZ and G-EAKZ were bought to work the South Wales beaches and it is believed that at least one of these worked from the beach at Porthcawl to the aerodrome at Locks Lane. Just a short trip, but what a take-off from the sands! So in 1920, Mssrs Holmes and a Captain Hamilton flew regular flights from Locks Common throughout the year until, on the 19 August, Capt. Hamilton flew away to Taunton, as the bad weather had ruined the company.

In November 1920 F.G.M. Sparkes and E.A. Sullock formed the Welsh Aviation Co. Ltd,to revive flying at Swansea, still taking place on Brynmill Sands. The company flew three Avro 504Ks – G-EAWK, G-EAWL and G-EAWM – and on 16 June 1921 the *Porthcawl News* announced that the Western Aviation Co. of Swansea had extended their services to Porthcawl on Saturdays, and would continue to make more flights on Wednesdays, Saturdays and Sundays during the season. On the Saturday a splendid exhibition was given by Capt. Broad flying a Sopwith Pup.

The Neath turf accountant Evan Williams bought out South Wales Aviation in April 1922 and the company served Porthcawl until 2 October 1922. On this date Evan Williams, his pilot, F. Bush, and a passenger were killed when G-EAWK crashed into the sea near Brynmill Sands, Swansea.

In May 1924, Mr Bernard Martin made an application to use the beach at Porthcawl for aeroplane flights. He had been doing the same at Cleethorpes and had had 19,000 passengers to commend him. Nothing came of this and the 1924 and 1925 seasons passed without much flying except the airshows.

South Wales Airways operated Avro 504s G-EBNH, G-EBSG, G-AASS, G-ABLV and G-ABLW during 1927. G-EBNH crashed at Bridgend on 7 May 1928 and the company bought G-EBSB, which was sold to Western Aviation in May 1928. The next purchase was G-AASS, which crashed in September 1931. G-ABLV was bought in May 1931 and scrapped in1936. Also in May 1931, G-ABLW was bought and struck off charge in 1934. Each of these aircraft in turn was kept at the hillside hangar at Wenvoe.

On 3 June 1932, Alan Cobham's 'Great Air Display' came to Locks Lane and was a huge success. The weather behaved and the show was outside the experience of all the people of Welsh towns, other than Cardiff or perhaps Wrexham. Twelve aircraft took part, with an event taking place every 15 minutes.

There were two new airliners (Airspeed Ferries), the autogyro and there was racing around pylons, aerobatics, including inverted flying seen for the first time outside the Hendon Air Display. The passenger rides, of course, were the money spinners from 4s upwards.

The following year, 1933, Sir Alan Cobham returned to Porthcawl with another show. This was to be at Crosshill Field on 24 May and at Locks Common on the 27th. Twenty events in the show would be held twice daily at 2.15 p.m. and 5.30 p.m. There was a parachutist, a miniature Schneider Trophy race, aerobatics in formation and wing walking with trapeze artists at 700ft, an autogyro and other new aircraft types. The following summer Cobham, in his 1934 tour, visited Cardiff, Barry, Port Talbot and Swansea, but not Porthcawl.

At the end of the 1934 season, during which time he had visited Cardiff and Swansea, Cobham sold his display without the right to use his name to C.W.A. Scott and Tom Campbell Black. This new company came to Locks Lane in 1936, under the title 'The British Empire Air Display'. The date was Sunday 2 July.

This RAF overhead of December 1946 shows all the places mentioned in this article. In the centre are the two fields used by Mr Pine. Below those are the hutted camp and cookhouse and below them the small field used as an airstrip by the US Army's Piper Cubs, with a tented camp at its eastern end. Houses cover the area now. (Welsh Assembly Photographic Archive)

Opposite below: An Airspeed Ferry G-ABSI at Locks Common in June 1932 with Cobham's Great Air Display.

This is an Avro 504K, as seen at Locks Common.

One of the aircraft of Welsh Aviation Co. seen at Locks Common many times in late 1920s and '30s.

Sir Alan Cobham at Locks Common in 1932 with his entourage and civic dignitaries. It was Aviation Day and the aircraft that they stand before was giving rides. It was a big aircraft for its day – the Handley-Page W10 G-EBMR.

The Cierva C19 Mk 1 G-ABGB, built in 1931 and delivered to Alan Cobham's National Aviation Day Displays Ltd in 1932. It is seen here at Locks Common in 1933.

During this display a Short Scion five-seater monoplane made a forced landing in a field near Locks Common, striking telephone wires on his way down, damaging the aircraft, bruising the five passengers and causing a compound fracture to the left leg of the pilot. This was Short Scion S16 2 G-ADTT.

George Stanley Pine at Locks
Common in 1938.

Also in 1936 was to come the advent that really made flying a regular thing. This was the arrival of Mr George Stanley Pine. He was a local, born in Newton, and after his schooling he helped his father who ran a taxi cab and funeral business, with horse-drawn hansom and two covered cabs. Later Mr Pine bought a Buick motorcar and started the Porthcawl Omnibus Co., using a converted Renault.

George Pine had trained at Marconi and made his own wireless sets, which he sold in the village. He joined the British Oxygen Co. to learn how to weld and he also went to Cardiff Airport to learn how to fly. He obtained his pilot's license 'A' and, in 1934, went to de Havilland at Hatfield to train for his 'B' licence. He bought his first plane, a Fox Moth, for £1,200. At first it was necessary for him to fly the aircraft to Cardiff every morning for a serviceability inspection, so George then qualified as an engineer in order that he could carry out his own checks at Porthcawl. He then, under the company title of Pines Airways, became quite a busy man. Operating from Locks Common, he offered up and down flights for 2s 6d, over Kenfig Pool 5s, Nash lighthouse £1, and a flight to Cardiff or Mumbles (Swansea) £2. So successful was this enterprise that George bought another Fox Moth. His first acquisition was G–ABVK and the second was G–ACEX, in February 1939 and December 1939, respectively. Both aircraft were shortly to be impressed into the wartime Air Transport Auxiliary (ATA) and neither was to survive for long. ABVK was scrapped on 19 August 1941 and ACEX on 6 April 1941, after overturning on landing at RAF Wroughton while flying with No.3 Ferry Pool.

In the last year of peace, Pines Airways flourished and the aerodrome attracted Alan Cobham, Amy Johnson and her husband Jim Mollison, and in the last week of August 1939 3,500 passengers were carried.

Mr Pine with G–ACEX, his second Fox Moth at Bristol (Whitchurch) in 1939.

George Pine's first Fox Moth G–ABVK, here at Locks Common, which he bought in June 1937 from Hillman Airways.

At the outbreak of war all civil flying was to cease and the aerodrome was closed. The two Moths were taken and Mr Pine joined the Air Transport Auxiliary, becoming one of the founder members of that organisation, based at Whitchurch (Bristol) Airport. After six years of service, and rising to second in command in the ATA, becoming captain, George and his colleagues were disbanded and sought other work. George received the MBE at Cardiff Castle from King George VI in 1945 for his wartime duties

After the war Mr Pine was unable to obtain the use of his former airfield for flying and he was offered work as a test pilot for an aircraft company near Birmingham. He decided that he was too old for test flying and instead he accepted a job in Blackpool. In 1946 he became one of the founder members of the Liverpool and Blackpool based charter company named Skytravel, becoming managing director of this company's Northern Division. Unfortunately, in the summer of 1947 the company failed and

This shot shows the old Locks Common, alongside Locks Lane. This photograph taken from what was the entrance gate to Locks Common. (Ivor Jones)

Locks Common today, looking north. None of the housing was here in pre-war Porthcawl. (Ivor Jones)

operations by Skytravel ceased, so Captain Pine decided to resume operations under the title of Pines Airways. In August 1947 he took over the two Austers formerly owned by Duke Joinery, which had previously been flown from Hooton Park. Captain Pine flew his aircraft to Blackpool and commenced charter passenger operations once more from there. Throughout the summer months these aircraft were used in the usual pleasure flights from Blackpool and other random charters, plus the occasional army cooperation contract, sometimes using Dragon Rapides of other Blackpool based companies such as Air Navigation and Trading or the Lancashire Aircraft Corporation. Captain Pine retained absolute control of his company as managing director, chief pilot and operations manager, and flourished well into the 1950s, but by the spring of 1955 all flying had ceased and the company's name disappeared.

The aerodrome at Locks Common was all grass, of course, and in plan view formed a capital 'L' in reverse. It was flanked on its south-east by the road Locks Lane, on its north-west side by the coast road leading to the Porthcawl Golf Club and to the large 'Rest House', a convalescent home for miners. This field was enlarged to the north by making a gap in the hedge, but in 1939 Mr Pine moved his airfield several hundred yards to the north and built a substantial hangar and office. Nobody can explain why this move was needed after so long, but it was not used for long before the war and the ultimate end of Locks Common Airfield. After the war housing encroached on a lot of this area, but because it is common land, a large part of the original field is still vacant.

After the beginning of hostilities, Porthcawl became a place that housed and billeted troops of all countries. Like most seaside resorts, accommodation was available and space to the opposite side of Locks Lane to the old aerodrome, in an area of thinly dispersed middle-class houses, a camp of Nissen huts was established that successively housed British, Dutch and American troops. It was while the British were in occupation that an accident occurred that is worth retelling, even if its aviation content is thin.

On 8 April 1942 ATS Private Lydia Amy Springs was leaving the cookhouse on this camp, after an early dinner, when an accidental discharge from a turret on Whitley K8942 killed her. It should be explained that this coastline was the patrol line for the target tugs and Gunnery School aircraft from Stormy Down, although this accident should not have happened, as the patrol lines should have been flying further out to sea.

Just a few hundred yards to the south-east of this army camp was one other place of interest. Another piece of land, surrounded on three sides by houses – and at the war's end itself to be built upon with fine houses – on the promenade, facing a lovely sea view, was another wartime memory. In early 1944 units of the US 28th Infantry Division arrived at Porthcawl, which was also the site of the L4s (Piper Cubs) of the 107th Field Artillery Battalion. The engineers of the battalion used the Nissen camp previously described and the Air Observation Post personnel used this patch of land to pitch their tents. It also provided the airstrip for the L4s. This lay on the inland side of the promenade, between the present Victoria Avenue and Severn Road (see photograph). The only trace of this American occupation is at the Nissen camp site, where an old rusty pipe set in concrete has the badge of the US engineers impressed and preserved. The unit badge was of a castle with three towers and can be seen on the grassy island in the road at Hutchwns Close. This iron pipe was once part of the same cookhouse that was to see the unfortunate demise of Miss Lydia Springs.

TWENTY-NINE

Airstrip at Margam Castle

Grid Reference SS 805860, off junction 38 of M4, near Port Talbot

The castle is built on a plateau on the slopes of the two hills, Graig Fawr and Mynedd y Castell, with a view to the west of the Bristol Channel and the steel works on Margam Moors. It also had a view of the bombing and gunnery ranges on the sands where the aircraft from nearby Stormy Down shot at ground targets or air to air firing during the war. There was a further connection with Stormy and the Margam Park during the conflict; on the crest of Graig Fawr was a radar mast and control under the command of RAF Stormy Down which was the fixing point on the bomb drop signals, where the target was moored off the coast on the ranges. This target was bombed with the utmost accuracy by units of the RAF and the USAAC in the early 1940s and was in the process of developing Britain's 'Oboe' navigation bombing aid.

The site was the place where a Cistercian Abbey was built in 1147, which, after being hit by the Black Death, fell into decline. Ruins of the abbey can still be seen. It was purchased by Sir Rice Mansell in 1540 who built a fine Tudor House nearby. When the family line ran out in the absence of a male heir, the estate was to go, through marriage, to the Talbot family whose descendants would demolish the Tudor house and build the castle in its place, with completion in 1840.

In 1918 the ownership of the estate changed on the death of Charlotte Talbot and came into the Fletcher family, one of whose sons was to build tennis courts, squash courts and a garage for motor cars where there had been stables. He also had an airplane and in the 1930s would take off and alight on the large area of lawns and woods to the rear of the castle. The same area that was to be used by American aircraft in a short time to come.

On the outbreak of the Second World War, the billeting of troops, British and foreign, at the castle was introduced, even while the Fletchers still lived there. In 1941 they sold the estate and returned to Saltoun Hall. The contents of the house were auctioned at Christies of London in a four-day sale, ending on 30 October 1941.

The estate was acquired by Mr D.M. Evans-Bevan (later Sir Evans-Bevan) in 1942, but he could not live in the castle as it was occupied by one unit or another up to the war's end.

In November 1943 the Americans arrived at the castle from Pembroke: the first Battalion of the 109th Field Artillery Regiment of the 28th Division (Pennsylvania National Guard).

The Piper Cub L4 Air Observation Post aircraft that came with the battalion was to use the field at the rear of the castle. Artillery and aircraft trained on the ranges that were abundant in Wales in preparation for the invasion of France. They were visited by General Eisenhower at the castle a few weeks before D-Day.

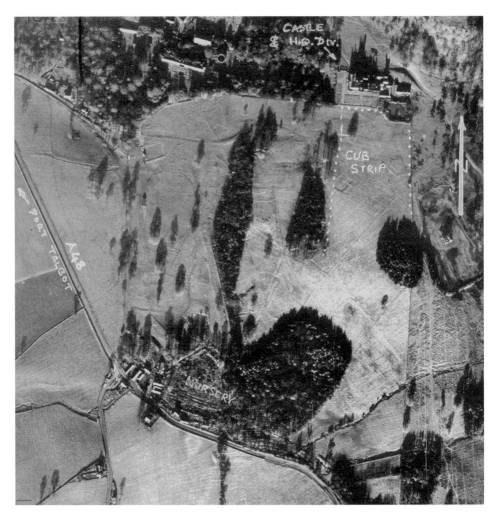

Margam Park with the old house at top right, 4 December 1946. There were a few flat areas of lawn that could have been used as a landing ground at Margam Castle park. That they did have a landing ground here is on record, but no one is able to state positively which lawn is the correct one. To me, even though there have been some changes made to the grounds, it would have been the area shown on the overhead. (Welsh Assembly Government Photographic Archive)

This is the area that must have been in use for the Piper Cubs. The proximity to the 28th Division artillery command, post residing in the castle 200m away, makes this lawn the obvious one. Note the miniature railway track that gives train rides in the summer.

Facing the castle at Margam, and standing on approximately the southern end of the cubstrip. The fields around this estate were accommodating tents for many troops of the US Army. (Ivor Jones)

The division moved a little closer to the embarkation points by leaving for the Swindon area in May 1944, and the accommodation was taken up by other allied units until the hostilities ceased. The place was left unoccupied for many years; the castle and its parks became dilapidated and abused by vandalism, because Mr Evans-Bevan still lived at Twyn yr Hydd.

In 1973 the estate was acquired by Glamorgan County Council and a start was made on recovering its former glory. Today it represents a good day out for anyone. Its ponds and gardens, abbey and church, and many ancient sites make for a pleasant walk

THIRTY

Jersey Marine Airport

Grid reference SS 712930, between Swansea and Neath, West Glamorgan

The millionaire Mr Whitney Straight purchased this area of land from the earl of Jersey to enable him to develop this landing ground into a terminus for his company, Western Airways, initially to run scheduled flights to Cardiff (Pengam Moors), and then connect with the company's services to Weston-Super-Mare and Bristol. The deal was completed on 14 July 1938; an Air Ministry licence to operate services out of Jersey Marine had been obtained.

Flying had begun from here three years earlier, when Captain C.D. Godfrey took over an option on land lying to the south of the Swansea Bay Golf Club and north of the dunes along the coast of the Nedd River estuary. Here started a long and worrying time for the club. C.D. Godfrey was a member of the club, and the owner of the land containing the golf club and the airfield was the president of the same club, the earl of Jersey, who encouraged Godfrey in his attempt to make an airfield out of his sandy piece of undeveloped land. Godfrey, a real character, a vigorous, brave and forward-thinking man who had risen to the rank of captain in the First World War, had obtained his pilot's licence in 1937 at the age of seventy, and regularly flew his aircraft (Tiger Moth) to London from Jersey Marine. His two sons, Paul and Michael, also won their pilots' licences and flew from this field, together with local businessmen of the area. They spent time and money filling holes and levelling, and made the strip safe and flat, encouraging visits by members of Cardiff Aero Club and Cardiff Flying Club, which became frequent in the summers of the late 1930s. It was in 1938 that Western Airways became part of the Straight Corporation and plans to enlarge the airstrip were first mooted, with visions of a large airfield to develop. The site at hand was approximately 1,400 yards long and 800 yards wide. Extensions would require levelling the dunes on the sea side and the encroachment of a substantial part of the greens of the golf club.

The site was a grass field running roughly west–east with a narrow strip of sand dunes between it and the sea at Swansea Bay. There was speculation in the press at the time that the size of this development would encroach further into the dunes and possibly further north into the Swansea Bay Golf Club. Club members were not in a position to complain about the threatened encroachment by the Straight Corporation as it was their own benefactor who was behind the development. Indeed the clubhouse and heavy roller of the golf course were in regular use by the airline, one as a terminal to shelter passengers on departure or arrival and the second to do the levelling out of the airstrip when needed.

Opposite, below: Jersey Marine Airport in 1938 looking from the golf course side of the single runway. Admittedly this photograph is of poor quality but it serves its purpose. Note the line of sand dunes along the Nedd estuary in the background.

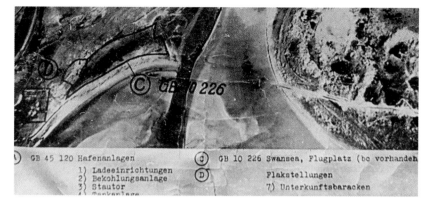

The Nedd (Neath) river estuary on 15 January 1941. Part of an overall on the Neath, Port Talbot, and Swansea target file. This shows the Nedd in the centre and the airfield of Jersey Marine on the left (outlined) and also the anti-aircraft sites, and barracks for the gun crews. The Germans knew of this airfield long before the war, as it was known as Swansea Airport. At the time of this Luftwaffe photograph the airfield was defunct and disused. (Welsh Assembly Government Photographic Archive)

The spot-on positioning of the runway here, as it was pre-war, is hard to define now as it was merely sea grass holding the sand dune material of river mud, fine pebble and fine sand as a foundation. Much road building parallel to it and the proximity of the golf course, plus sea wall alterations, have totally confused the attempt to align the old with the new. The white line is my best guess. (Welsh Assembly Government Photographic Archive)

It is difficult today to assess the total area, as no records remain. There are no plans or overhead photographs and this is explained by the fact that the history of the place was so brief. It would appear that the extensions did not take place. In early 1939 the plans were issued that would have reduced the size of the course considerably but a stay of execution was arranged to enable a Ladies Welsh Championship Tournament to take place at Swansea Bay, as it had been arranged a long time in advance. Expansion was delayed until after the contest and before they could resume their plan after that, the threat of war gradually intervened in their deliberations.

The militia and other territorial units had always used these large flat fields for drill, exercise and parade, and there were rifle ranges to the western end of the future airfield with barracks. During the Second World War this area was home to several batteries of anti-aircraft guns.

The dual carriageway A483 runs alongside the runway's length on its way west to Swansea, but this was not laid until long after the war. This road did far more damage to the golf course than the airfield did. Built in 1947, it sliced through several greens and holes, and it was not until 1955 that the full eighteen holes were reconstructed here.

Airline services started after a flight was arranged to carry the Mayor of Swansea and chairman of Neath Council to Weston for lunch in a DH Dragon. The Swansea Chamber of Commerce expressed its pleasure to Mr Straight for the fine start to a new airport for its citizens. The schedule would be Cardiff to Swansea, arriving at 9.55 a.m. and leave again five minutes later for the return journey. The evening flight was to arrive at 7.55 p.m. and leave for Cardiff at 8 p.m.; the journey time was 12 minutes. These flights were timed to connect with the Weston and other services.

A new hangar/shed was erected at the west end of the strip. No photographs or drawings of it exist, but a couple of mens who were youths at the time remember it as medium sized and steel, with Western Airways painted across the roof. A manager was engaged to handle the 'airport' and was none other than the boss of the Bluebird Bus Co. of Neath. Mr Straight's takeover of Jersey Marine was only the latest of airport acquisitions: Western Airways had been running a Cardiff to Weston and Cardiff to Bristol service, and making a profit when the Straight Corporation Ltd took over in January 1938. They had held an interest since 1937 and with the complete takeover began the expansion that was intended to make every town in the UK – especially the south-west – acquire an aerodrome with a view to linking each to another in a bus stop service on both sides of the Bristol Channel. Subsidiary bases were set up at Whitchurch in Bristol, Exeter and Plymouth. The group also operated the airports at Ramsgate, Ipswich, and Inverness.

This man – Whitney Willard Straight - was only twenty-five years old when he took over Western Airways. He first flew solo at the age of sixteen and obtained his full licence a year later. He was also an excellent motor racing driver. Six months after his takeover

Opposite, centre: Western Airways' DH 84 Dragon G-ACMJ at Jersey Marine. Note the chimneys and smoke stacks of the Port Talbot steelworks across the river Neath to the east. (Welsh Assembly Government Photographic Archive)

Opposite, below: This Western Airways DH 86B Express was operating the route Jersey –Cardiff– Weston-Super-Mare. This much larger aircraft which was deemed necessary to meet the demand, from April 1939 until the outbreak of the Second World War, saw the permanent end of this unknown airport.

Above: Believed to be the flight that transported the Mayor and the Chairman of Neath Council to Weston for lunch in 1938. The Swansea Chamber of Commerce were also there for this inauguration from Jersey Marine.

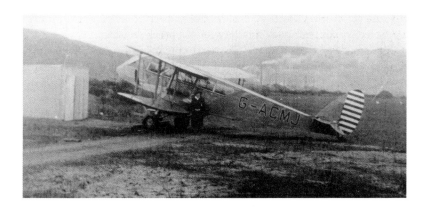

of Western Airways he was inaugurating his first flights from Jersey Marine and the company was operating with a fleet of DH 84 Dragons and DH 89 Rapides, one of these being G-ADDD, the first aircraft used by the King's Flight RAF upon its formation in 1936. The Prince of Wales considered the aircraft his own.

Provisional licences were issued to Western Airways in October 1938 for routes between Weston-Super-Mare and Cardiff, and Weston-Super-Mare and Swansea. December brought about the publication of a Government White Paper giving details of proposed subsidies available to internal airlines. A maximum of £100,000 would be available in any one year and Western eventually received a subsidy for its routes.

On 8 May 1939 Western Airways started a Manchester to Penzance service, calling at Barnstaple Airport. On the same day, a twice daily Swansea (Jersey Marine) –Barnstaple– Newquay (Trebelzue) –Penzance (St Just) service began, operating with DH 84s

In April 1939 DH 86b Express was purchased from Allied Airways to help cope with the expected increase in traffic on the Cardiff/Weston route, and passengers were brought from Jersey Marine to feed this service. Demand was such that over the five days of Whitsun 2,555 passengers were carried from Weston Aerodrome allowing the company to claim a world record.

The Western Airways flights timetable from Jersey Marine in the last summer before the war – 1939 – rose to five daily departures from Swansea to Bristol via Cardiff leaving at 9.20 a.m., 12 p.m., 4.20 p.m., 6.20 p.m. and 8.20 p.m., returning from Cardiff at 9.45 a.m., 12.25 p.m.,4.45 p.m., 6.45 p.m. and 8.45 p.m. The first three of these connected at Bristol to Western's services to Birmingham and Manchester.

There were five flights originating from Bristol and they departed Cardiff for Jersey Marine at 8.50 a.m., 11.30 a.m., 2.50 p.m., 5.50 p.m. and 7.50 p.m., two of which – 8.50 a.m. and 5.50 p.m. – continued on to Barnstaple. The 11.30 a.m. departure continued on beyond Barnstaple to Newquay and Penzance.

So it seemed at the time that aviation was booming and money was being made by internal airlines, but then the war arrived on 3 September 1939 and, under an agreement with the Air Ministry, the aircraft belonging to the airlines were impressed into the National Air Communications Organisation. For some obscure reason Western was able to resume the Weston to Cardiff route, but by 1940 all the aircraft were impressed into RAF service. The DH 86B Express was intended to be commandeered into the RAF but political moves to help the Finnish government in their defence against the USSR meant the aircraft was passed to Finland as it was not a 'warplane'. It left on 3 December for service with the Finnish Naval Coastguard Service as an air ambulance and was destroyed on the ground at Malmi on 2 May 1940.

During the period of partial impressments one of the directors of Western Airways, Mr Leslie Arnott, crashed one of the Dragons – G-ACJT – and was killed. The company received compensation for all their aircraft two years later.

During 1939 Whitney Straight had become a pilot officer in the RAF with No.501 Squadron Royal Auxiliary Air Force and was to serve with great distinction, earning the MC, DFC and CBE.

At the end of the war flying resumed. In May 1948 Western Airways was granted a British European Airways associate agreement for the operation of a scheduled passenger service between Weston and Cardiff, in association with Cambrian Air Services, but Jersey Marine was never reactivated after the war, as all flying was to be from ex-RAF Fairwood Common.